Half Time

In memory of my mother Mair
1946-2009

and to my father Geraint for all his love and support

Half Time

Nigel Owens
The Autobiography

with Lynn Davies

y Lolfa

First impression: 2009
Fourth impression: 2014

The publishers wish to acknowledge the support of
Cyngor Llyfrau Cymru

Photographs courtesy of the author unless noted otherwise.

Cover photograph: Warren Orchard
Cover design: Y Lolfa

ISBN: 9781847711328
Paperback ISBN: 9781847712011

Printed on acid-free and partly recycled paper
and published and bound in Wales by
Y Lolfa Cyf., Talybont, Ceredigion SY24 5HE
e-mail ylolfa@ylolfa.com
website www.ylolfa.com
tel 01970 832 304
fax 832 782

April 1996

It's half past three in the morning. I got up about an hour ago so that my parents wouldn't see me leaving the house. I hope they're still asleep so that I can do what I have to do. I've left a note telling them that I've reached the end of my tether and that the only solution for me now is to take my own life.

So many things have been playing on my mind for so long. I enjoy life but I have this obsession that I look obscenely fat, with the result that I have been suffering from bulimia for many years. I've also been going regularly to the gym to try and replace fat with muscle. In order to speed up that process, I began taking steroids and became hooked. They caused many side effects which, I'm sure, have contributed to my being in this particular place at this particular time.

There are so many positive aspects to my life, yet I'm feeling depressed and have been for some time. But I'm unable to tell anyone. The main reason for my despair is that I'm thoroughly unhappy with the type of person that I have become. There's another person inside me trying to get out but he doesn't know how. I'm gay but I don't know what to do about it. I don't want to be gay, and during the last few years I have tried so hard not to be. I feel that there's only one thing left for me to do, and that is to end my life before people find out about me.

I've come to the top of Bancyddraenen Mountain which overlooks the village of Mynyddcerrig where I've lived all my life. I have a number of sleeping tablets with me and I intend to take an overdose so that I can be rid of all my problems. In case the tablets don't work, I also have a shotgun.

October 2009

On looking back at that terrible chapter in my life, I can't believe that I sank into such a pit of despair. It came about because I was unable to accept who and what I am, but I will never allow myself to reach that state again. Since that time I've found so much pleasure in pursuing such rewarding and successful careers, both as a referee and as an entertainer. In addition I've received much valuable support and friendship from family and acquaintances. Never again will I put them through such hell. I very much hope, therefore, that *Half Time* will not only be an interesting read but will also provide comfort and inspiration for people who are having to face up to some of the problems that were such a burden to me in the past. I, thankfully, was able to overcome them.

CHAPTER 1

Roots

As A CHILD I always wanted to be a farmer. Until I was about five years old, I lived with my parents on a smallholding called Moultan, in the village of Mynyddcerrig (literally 'mountain of stone') in the Gwendraeth Valley in south west Wales. Coal mining was the main source of employment in the area before the industry's demise during the latter part of the last century, and to this day the Welsh language is often the medium of communication. Also living at Moultan were my grandmother, my grandfather and Uncle Ken, my father's brother. He was one of seven children, all of whom had been brought up there, and the family were commonly referred to in the village as the 'Moultan Family'. My grandparents, Wil and Maggie Moultan, were from farming stock. During my early years they worked some three acres of land there as well as renting a further eight acres, owned by Mrs Rees, Bancyreos, in order to raise horses. My earliest memories, as a three-year-old, are of visiting those fields to care for four-legged friends such as Susie, Bet, Fred and Cara. My grandparents also kept two or three cows and would sell a little milk and butter to friends and neighbours. There's no doubt, therefore, that my interest in farming stemmed from those early days I spent on the fields of Moultan and at the place we called the Gagal where we would keep our horses most of the time.

Farming was also in the blood on my mother's side of the family. Both her parents, Lyn and Maud Nicholas, were brought up on farms, my grandmother being one of ten children raised at Upper Marchoglwyn, in Pontyberem, while my grandfather had nine brothers and sisters, all of whom were brought up at Hirwaun Olaf in the village of Tumble. Unfortunately both passed away before I had the chance to get to know them. Lyn was killed in a car crash when my mother was fourteen years old. My grandmother suffered from ill-health with the result that my mother, being the eldest child that was still living at home, bore the responsibilities of running the house and becoming the sole breadwinner from a very early age. That difficult time served, no doubt, to make her the most loving and wonderful mother I could have wished for, and the way in which she looked after my father and me was remarkable.

Perhaps what stimulated my interest in farming most was that Tir Garn farm bordered on Moultan and provided a welcome retreat during my childhood and early teenage years. I recall fleeing up to Tir Garn through a hole in the hedge at every opportunity, with the result that Dewi and Dilys, who farmed there, had to shout down to the family at Moultan on a regular basis in order to let them know where I was, as we didn't have a telephone at the time – in fact I was about fourteen years old before we had one. Then, when I was about five years old, my parents and I moved to a council house in the centre of the village: Number 8, Maeslan Estate.

I am so proud of my roots at Maeslan. It was a very special community which gave me such a strong sense of identity. Neighbours and families looked out for each other and friendships were formed which have remained to this day, even amongst people who rarely have a chance to meet. My father still lives there, and the only thing that seems to have changed is that the language spoken by some of the residents is English. Consequently, the children rarely speak Welsh on the street nowadays, although most of them can speak it fluently.

Half the properties there are now owned privately, including my father's house. My parents bought it in 1980 by taking advantage of the scheme introduced by Mrs Thatcher's government. Our family, like most in the Gwendraeth Valley, were opposed to Mrs Thatcher and her policies, but we were indeed grateful for that particular legislation, which gave us our only chance of becoming homeowners.

The only time my parents, grandparents and I would place a bet on the horses would be on the occasion of the Grand National. One particular year I chose a horse called Grittar, not because the name had any particular appeal but because it was horse number eight and we lived at number eight. As it happened, it won, and ever since I have regarded eight as a kind of lucky number. For example, I bet on number eight in the Grand National each year (although I have never won a penny since Grittar galloped home!). I once bought a number plate with '8' on it. It was to go on my first sports car, a Ford Cougar which I purchased at the age of 29 from a local garage managed by my cousin, Eifion. He said that the car would suit me! However, the rest of the plate was perhaps even more significant, for the whole thing read '8 REF'!

For many years I would disappear every Saturday and during school holidays to work at Tir Garn, where I really enjoyed tasks such as fencing, baling or cleaning out the cowshed. Even more pleasing was the fact that I was always made to feel like one of the family by Dewi, Dilys and their daughters, Angharad, Rhiannon and Naomi. The mainstay of the farm was rearing beef cattle, and working with the animals really appealed to me. However, apart from taking great pleasure in driving the tractor at all times, I had no interest whatsoever in farm machinery, and that still applies today. It was only a small farm of just over forty acres, which wasn't enough to keep Dewi fully employed. So every day he worked at the local quarry, Torcoed, which he reached by walking for a mile or so across the fields.

The highlight of the year for me would be the hay harvest, when all the Tir Garn family would get together to bring in thousands of small bales. Howard and Elvie from Y Wern farm, for example, would be baling all day long, while I and the rest of the Tir Garn family, which included Dewi's brothers, nephews and brother in law, would be collecting the hay. There was a lot of fun and leg-pulling amidst all the hard work, particularly when we all sat around the table afterwards for a hearty supper. This group usually consisted of Dewi's brothers, Elwyn and Gareth, Rhodri and his wife, Annie Mary, their son Emyr, Andrew (Elwyn's son) and Mona. I was paid £5 by Dewi every time I went to Tir Garn, regardless of whether I was busy or not, so I didn't dream of doing anything else during my leisure time in those days, as £5 was a lot of money then, especially for a kid like me. When there were slack periods on the farm I would take the dogs out on the mountain. I'm not sure whether it was I or they who took the greatest pleasure from those occasions.

From time to time, during school holidays, I would escape to Pentwyn farm in the nearby village of Llannon to stay with Gloria, my grandmother's sister, and her husband Graham. I would stay sometimes for a week, or even a fortnight, and would really enjoy myself in their company, in particular with their children, Janet, Gillian, Jane and Andrew – the latter being the same age as me. It was there that I learned how to drive a tractor and it was while at Pentwyn that I went with the family to the Royal Welsh Agricultural Show for the first time. It is a huge event and for most people the highlight of the Welsh agricultural calendar. Whilst there I managed to get lost, with the result that I was deposited in tears at the Lost and Found stand, to the sound of the PA system's earnest appeal that whoever had 'lost' Nigel Owens should come and collect him! The experience had been so frightening that quite some time went by before I paid my another visit to the Royal Welsh, which was when I promoted refereeing on the Welsh Rugby Union (WRU) stand. Then, in 2009, I recorded a Welsh radio programme there, which was part of a series I presented on the Young Farmers movement, produced by the BBC and Telesgop, an independent company. For the forseeable future

I'm glad to say that I shall have an even closer involvement with the movement, since, in September, I was invited to become President of the Wales Federation of Young Farmers. I consider this to be a tremendous honour, bestowed by those who represent the future of agriculture and rural communities in Wales, and I look forward to undertake my duties in that respect and to give a little back to a movement that I've had so much out of.

Naturally, I've had a love of horses ever since I was a small boy. As well as breeding ponies, my father and grandfather also broke them in. They would begin by putting a saddle on the pony's back, before getting me, at the next stage, to ride it for a while. Then one of them would take to the saddle to complete the process. When a horse was taken along the road to better pastures, I would always be allowed to ride it bareback – which at times could be quite a task! We would usually like a pony to get used to having someone in the saddle when it was about two years old. I remember on one such occasion, riding in one of the fields which bordered on the road when a passing car sounded its horn. The pony reared up on its hind legs and began to fall backwards, but luckily my grandfather was alert to the situation and snatched me from the saddle before the horse hit the ground. That incident, however, didn't in any way detract from the great pleasure I derived from working with the horses.

I still fondly remember the significance of certain dates in the horse calendar. I recall going with my parents and grandfather to the Llanybydder horse fair and taking ponies to be sold at the Llandovery fair in July, where my grandfather, on one occasion, bought a pony for £25 which he then groomed and trained for a year before selling it for £250. I still have a great interest in horses which these days, unfortunately, I'm not able to actively pursue. When life becomes less hectic, perhaps when I have finished travelling all over the world, I would love to have a smallholding with a field or two where I could breed horses. Even better if that place were Moultan.

To a great extent the Gwendraeth Valley was an industrial area. My grandfather on my mother's side, like most of his generation, was a collier, as was my other grandfather who also farmed a little. His life was indeed hard, since he would have to get up at four o'clock in the morning to milk the cows before walking to the pit. My father worked for a while as a coal miner and in the washery above ground, but for most of his life he was a quarryman in Crwbin and at Torcoed in Mynyddcerrig. He was unemployed occasionally, but through thick and thin my parents always ensured that I never wanted for anything.

The way I was raised by my grandparents and Uncle Ken has also had a great influence on me. The standards which they considered important have served as a benchmark for me and, to some extent, their interests have influenced my personal tastes, with the result that I could perhaps be deemed old fashioned in some ways. For example, my grandmother's favourite record, 'Tecel', sung by the Welsh group Hogia'r Wyddfa, is also one of my favourites, and the hymn that she liked best, 'Pantyfedwen', which was sung at her funeral in 1994, would be my first choice. On that occasion the congregation, which took up every available seat in the chapel at Capel Seion, also sang the hymn 'O fy Iesu Bendigedig', and I shall remember the emotional impact of those hymns that day for the rest of my life. I was very close to my grandmother and the occasion was rather too much for me in that I cried throughout the service.

The family is all important to us. Since my father was one of seven children and my mother one of six, I have eighteen cousins who have been very much a part of my life. Some are quite a bit older than me, but in general we have always kept in constant touch with each other. As a boy I was particularly close to some of them, such as Helen, whose father Emrys was my father's brother, and Ceirwen, who lived next door for years and who was like a sister to me. I also thought the world of Uncle Ken who was always there for me, particularly when I wanted a chauffeur!

It is often said that life is what you make it, but in my opinion it is life that makes you. The way you are brought up by your parents, the family that surrounds you from day to day, the friends that have grown up with you and the society of which you are a part, all have an important contribution in making you the person that you are. I have been able to draw upon all of these and I am extremely fortunate in having a very special family about me, both young and old.

My immediate family used to go on holiday with Helen's family every year, usually to a caravan in Pendine on the Carmarthenshire coast, and we would have a great time there. On one particular occasion when a married couple from Aberdare had come to stay in the next caravan to ours, the husband took me fishing to a nearby beach. I managed to catch a bass of respectable size which was the very first fish that I had caught and which served as our supper in the caravan that night. But more importantly, perhaps, the experience whetted my appetite for similar opportunities after going home. Indeed I started to fish regularly in the Gwendraeth Fach river which flowed through Glanrynys, farmed by Dewi, one of my grandfather's friends. Ken and my father often used to come with me and ever since those days I have enjoyed river fishing. Sadly, however, I've had little opportunity to do this in recent years.

We also went on holiday to Butlins in Pwllheli on one or two occasions, which were my first visits to North Wales. Apart from enjoying the usual holiday camp activities such as the Donkey Derby (I had some success as a jockey on one occasion), there were also opportunities to see some of the surrounding countryside and, even more importantly perhaps for a lad from the Gwendraeth Valley, to experience the magic of places like Beddgelert.

My days at the little Mynyddcerrig school were very happy, although you wouldn't have thought as much from my first visit there, when I clung to my father's hand and cried so much that he brought me back home to Moultan. He comforted me by promising that I didn't have to go to school if I didn't want to. But my mother's reaction was quite the opposite. After giving us both a piece of her mind, my father and I had to do an immediate about-turn and make our way back to the school. When I started there it had 17 pupils, but in a year or two the number increased to 25 since some English families moved into the area. This led to English replacing Welsh as the language of the schoolyard.

We had such a lot of fun in Mynyddcerrig school in the care of two teachers, Mr Wyn Gravell and Miss Margaret Tunichie, a lovely lady who lived nearby in Drefach and who attended the same chapel as me. She was my teacher until I reached the age of seven, whereupon I moved up to Mr Gravell's class, where I remained until I left Mynyddcerrig school at the age of eleven. He was a strict teacher, but very fair, although I seemed to get into trouble with him quite often. I recall having a ruler, and once even a cricket bat, across my backside for misbehaving in class and for not doing my work as I should. He always told my mother that I was intelligent enough to do well at school but that I was more interested in playing the fool and being mischievous. Regardless of my mother's efforts to help me to do my homework, my priority at such times would be to get out of the house to play with my mates in Maeslan.

I had some great friends at junior school, such as Neil Williams (who sadly passed away in his early twenties), Christopher Lloyd, Gareth Davies, Michael Royals, my cousin Helen, Angharad Tir Garn, Avril Novello, Christian Murphy, Heidi Williams and Mark Lloyd. We were all big mates, apart from the time I annoyed one of the girls, Linda Norrie, so much when trying to get her to lend me her pencil, that in frustration she turned around and stabbed me in the chest with it. I had to go and see the local doctor in order to make sure that no lead had got into my bloodstream, and the pencil mark is still visible on my chest today. We both got told off: me for provoking her and her for GBH!

I have to confess that school activities such as singing in the morning service, acting in pantomimes and taking part in the annual nativity play appealed much more to me than academic pursuits. I didn't like reading much, apart from the occasional comic. To some it was no surprise to learn that Dennis the Menace was a particular hero of mine and I recall sending for a special badge which confirmed that I was a member of his fan club. In fact it's only during the last few years that I've taken to reading books, and that's due to the fact that I spend so much time travelling in planes and kicking my heels in airports and hotels. My favourite type of book would be Nelson Mandela's autobiography, in which he describes his life history and his fight against prejudice and injustice. Apart from the fact that he's so well respected all over the world for his achievements, I had the pleasure of meeting him when I officiated as a touch judge in a game between South Africa and Australia which he attended as part of his 86th birthday celebrations. Another reason I enjoyed that particular book so much was that my duties as a referee have enabled me to travel quite a lot in South Africa and to see many of the places to which he refers.

When I passed the 11+ examination to go to Gwendraeth Grammar School, I was the last pupil to do so from our village school before all secondary schools in the county became Comprehensive. I would probably have failed that exam were it not for the extra coaching in mathematics that I got from Lloyd, my father's cousin, who lived in the neighbouring village of Bancffosfelen with his wife Val and their children Richard and Jane (Louise was a late addition). My mother and Val were good friends, and had been since the day they both went to work at Woolworths in Carmarthen upon leaving school. Lloyd had a milk-round so he had to be good at sums. Yet although he was responsible to a large extent for my successful performance in the 11+ exam, I have to confess that the greatest incentive for me to go to Bancffosfelen for special lessons was the fact that I enjoyed the family's company there so much. Perhaps that which gave me greatest pleasure was having the opportunity to roam Bancffosfelen with Richard and his friends and getting up to all kinds of mischief.

Mynyddcerrig was a very small village. During my childhood the only institutions of any importance were the chip shop (which burned down when I was about five years old), the post office, the school and the working men's club. The club had a central role in the social life of the village. On occasions such as carnival day, whole families, including ours, would join in. My mother was a member of the village welfare committee and as such would be involved in organising the carnival each year. That was certainly the biggest event in the social calendar of the village and everybody who lived there would take part in some capacity or other. People from neighbouring areas, particularly those with families and friends in Mynyddcerrig, would make an effort to attend.

One carnival was instrumental in providing an important lesson in my moral development. Each year there would be a competition, held some weeks before the carnival day itself, to choose a 'Prince Charming' for the event. I never won, of course, but I did come close one year when I was selected as one of the 'Prince's Attendants'. However, what was particularly upsetting for me was that the person chosen as the Prince that year, Wyn Jones, was now living in the village of Drefach, although he used to live in number 5 Maeslan at one time. I complained bitterly to my mother that those who were not residents of Mynyddcerrig should not be allowed to compete in the Prince Charming competition, to which she replied that winning, although a pleasant experience, was not all-important and that one should also learn to accept coming second or third. This taught me a very valuable lesson, that one should not be jealous of someone else's good fortune or good looks as it was in this case.

One of the lasting memories I have of carnival day was the occasion when we all competed as a family in the fancy dress competition. I went as a collier, carrying my grandfather's helmet and lamp and wearing miners' clothes, with boot polish on my face to provide additional authenticity. My mother and Auntie Caerwen went as the TV sitcom duo George and Mildred, complete with bike and side-car, borrowed from my Uncle Irfon, my mother's brother. However, the star turns were my father, who went as Hilda Ogden from *Coronation Street*, and Robert Owen, who lived at 10 Maeslan, who went as Stan Ogden. They looked hilarious, particularly since my father is rather small and slight, with extremely thin, white legs whilst the 22-year-old Robert weighed in at 24 stone and was 6ft tall. Needless to say they took the first prize. Robert was a naturally funny man and a gentle giant who became a very good friend of mine until, sadly, he passed away in his early thirties.

From five o'clock onwards on the evening of the carnival, almost all the families would congregate in the club where there would be a lot of singing and laughing. With 'Nancy Piano' (as she was generally known) on the organ, a good night was had by all. My friends Christopher Lloyd, Neil Williams and I often sang in school and chapel concerts, but we always made an effort to appear at the club on carnival day, for there was a general consensus that if you received a favourable reception there, then you'd made it.

Towards the end of the night, when he'd had a few drinks, my father always ventured on stage to sing 'Lili Marlene'. He is not perhaps the best singer but he was always in demand with that particular number and invariably got rapturous applause. It's a sign of the times that there is no longer a village carnival, and not even an organ in the club. However they do have an occasional sing-song there, particularly when Tony Rees and

17

I are present.

In those boyhood days singing was my favourite leisure interest. Every month, in the children's service held at Seion Chapel in the next village, Christopher, Neil and I would perform solos and would also sing as a trio. We would do the same in local hymn-singing festivals and sometimes in Sunday school, which used to be held at Nebo Chapel in Mynyddcerrig every Sunday afternoon. We had three teachers there: Jimmy Tegfan, Joyce 'Mountain Gate' and Mrs Evans, Brynhawddgar.

It was probably Jimmy who first instilled in me the desire to perform in front of an audience. He was the one who got me to do so for the very first time, when I was three-and-a-half years old. He called at the house, carrying a Bible, and asked my mother whether I would be willing to read a few verses in the service at Sunday school. My mother was a little concerned that I wasn't old enough or sufficiently talented to undertake the task in question. However, Jimmy got her to agree, with the assurance that 'with practice he'll be fine'. My mother was probably more nervous than me but it all went very well, and when the minister, the Rev. Tudur Lloyd Jones (the father of Gwyn Elfyn, an actor in the popular Welsh soap, which is the longest-running TV soap in the UK and still going strong) specifically praised my contribution she was, I think, very proud.

I regularly attended Sunday school until I was thirteen years old, and during that period I often won the prize awarded annually to the pupil who had been absent on the fewest number of occasions. In due course there was no other pupil there of my age, so I too decided to leave. There is no longer a Sunday school at Nebo and the chapel building has now been bought by a local farmer. Even though I don't go to chapel any more (and I know that I should), I still feel that children today are losing out considerably by not going to Sunday school as we used to. A lot of the values and principles I hold today were taught to me at Sunday school and chapel. I think society and young people today would benefit immensely by attending Sunday school and chapel now and again. It's no wonder that children and young people in Wales no longer know the words of our most popular hymns.

It seems that tales of our singing talents in the local chapels had spread throughout the area, because on Saturday evenings, John Morgan and his wife Heulwen, who had recently taken over the Prince pub in the neighbouring village of Porthyrhyd, often sent a car up to Mynyddcerrig to fetch Christopher and me to entertain their customers. Christopher would also play the organ there and I would contribute some of the songs that I had learned in school and at Sunday school. Apart from the fact that I really enjoyed singing in front of an audience, the customers at the pub would also give me money, so my desire to perform was even greater!

There was also another pub where, as a lad of about ten, I tried my hand at entertaining the customers. Early each Friday evening my parents, my grandfather and I used to call at the Bridge Inn in the village of Cwmmawr, which was kept by my cousin Alan Rees and his wife Janet who had two children around my age, Stuart and Donna. Sometimes I would sing a solo or two in the bar and I remember Bill Tunichie (the father of Margaret, our teacher at Mynyddcerrig School) asking me to sing one evening and then taking his hat around the customers so that I would get some money for my efforts. It was quite a pleasant surprise to find afterwards that there was about £6 in the hat. Usually my mother and I would leave the Bridge after a while in order to visit the many relatives that we had in the area. My father and my grandfather, however, would move on to the Legion in Pontyberem where they usually enjoyed a game of bingo.

I always looked forward to those Friday nights and to visiting various members of the family. After dropping my father and grandfather off at the bingo, my mother and I would usually call to see her sister Gaynor, her husband Berian and their son

Meurig, who was a little younger than me. Then we would go and see another sister, Petula, her husband Keith and their children Wynn, Louise and Angharad. In the summer, Meurig, Wynn and I would join my other cousins, Adrian, Kevin and Wayne who were the sons of my mother's brother, David, to play games and create mischief around Pontyberem. When it was time to leave, my mother and I would collect my father and grandfather from the Legion and then call in to the local fish and chip shop for our supper, which we took home with us.

Sometimes the pattern varied and we would visit my father's sister Eiry and her husband, Hubert, before going on to see my mother's other sister Janice and her family in the village of Ponthenri. When I was young I spent a lot of time in Ponthenri with my cousin Carol and her son Jarret, who was some five years younger than me. Her husband, Alan, was a hero of mine, since he was captain of the Pontiets rugby team and would always be kicking a rugby ball about with Jarret and me.

Alan would often take us fishing in the Gwendraeth Fawr river that runs through the Gwendraeth Valley on its way to the sea at Cydweli and Pembrey. I suspect that we weren't always licensed to fish there because I recall on one occasion Alan telling us to remember to walk quietly and not to make too much noise if we caught anything! As a result, Jarret got so nervous that he didn't look where he was going and he fell into an old well – up to his waist in dirty, muddy water. The outcome was an abandoned fishing trip!

When I was 12 years old both my grandfather, at the age of 78, and my father's sister, Nancy, passed away within a short time of each other. My aunt's death, at a comparatively young age, was a great shock for the family. The week I was born, my grandfather had suffered a huge stroke and, although he battled back bravely to overcome its worst effects, it left him slightly impaired for the rest of his life. By the time of his death, he, along with my grandmother and Ken, had moved to the nearby village of Drefach, but they remained a significant influence on my life. Yet despite the very high regard I had for my grandfather, I announced that I didn't wish to go to his funeral. Indeed, during that period I went to stay with Dewi and Dilys at Tir Garn. It was as if I couldn't face the fact that he was now dead and that arrangements had to be made for his funeral. But at the last minute I telephoned my mother to say that I wanted to go to the funeral after all. Of course it was by then too late to ferry me from Tir Garn and for me to get changed and so on. As a result I spent the afternoon lying on my bed, crying my eyes out. Perhaps one of the reasons that I hadn't wanted to go initially was that I still remembered going to the only other funeral that I had ever been to when I was seven years old. That was the funeral of Mrs Evans, Brynhawddgar, one of my Sunday school teachers at the time, and I had cried throughout the service. After my grandfather's death I would often go to stay with my grandmother at Drefach. She was trying to come to terms with the blow of losing her daughter and her husband within a short time of each other. Yet she continued to delight in telling tales about the old days when she used to work on some of the local farms, and I would love to listen to her.

Sport didn't play that great a part in my life when I was young. As children, when we wanted something to do, we would go for a walk together to the top of the valley. There we would engage in some of the usual adventurous pursuits, such as climbing trees and sometimes building a house in the branches, not to mention riding the two donkeys that were kept on the farm which bordered on the Maeslan estate. There was always the urge to make innocent mischief, like walking across the land of a local farmer whom we knew would lose his temper and chase anyone who would do such a thing. Or perhaps we would place branches across one of the roads, thus forcing those driving by to get out of their vehicles to remove them whilst we, from a hiding place nearby, would delight in jeering and cheering their efforts. Come September we would take to stealing apples and would often derive great pleasure from throwing them high into the air so that they landed noisily on the roofs of the neighbouring houses. I remember once when it was my turn to throw, my misdirected apple resulted in a smashed garage window. I was caught and got into terrible trouble. It didn't stop me from stealing apples but that was the last time I attempted to bombard local houses with them!

Mynyddcerrig school was too small to have its own rugby team so two or three of us used to join the pupils of Drefach school to play an occasional game. I remember our first game against Cross Hands on the Cefneithin Rugby Club field (where heroes like Carwyn James and Barry John had played before me), when I scored my first try in a competitive game. I was playing number eight and from a scrum some ten metres out I picked the ball up and more or less strolled across the try line. I scored a similar try shortly afterwards, but I have to confess that I had no real idea of what I was doing at the time. In those days I was fairly well built, and at that particular level my size could be quite an advantage.

Our village didn't have a rugby team but was traditionally a soccer area. My father had been a member of the successful Mynyddcerrig team which, at the end of the 1950s, was able to attract three bus loads of supporters to see them play in the final of a local cup competition in Drefach Felindre. When I was a young lad we played soccer to amuse ourselves – sometimes in the local park where the old soccer pitch had been located, or on a patch of grass in the centre of the village. It was only after taking up the oval ball game at Gwendraeth Grammar School that we began to play rugby in the village, and before long we were playing as much rugby as soccer.

Of course, as a boy, I loved to watch the Wales rugby team on television and I remember the exact moment when

I thought to myself, 'Gosh, I like this rugby!' It was when Phil Bennett scored that fantastic try at Murrayfield in 1977, after side-stepping his way beautifully over the try line and lying on the ball under the posts with a little smile of satisfaction on his face. But I rarely had an opportunity to go to rugby matches until I was about thirteen years old, when my father and two family friends, Robert and Cyril Owen, would regularly take me to see Tumble, one of the best sides in the West Wales Ruby Union at the time, playing at home and away. I became good friends with other supporters, such as Simon Lewis and Leighton John, a nephew of Barry John, whose father, Clive, and uncle Alan (Barry's brothers) were the coaches of the Tumble team. Back then, during the early and mid 1980s, they played some great rugby with stars such as Tonto, Peris and Gareth in the back row, and Arwel dictating matters behind the scrum, in addition to the ever-reliable Wynford Lewis at full-back. Another reason for supporting Tumble was that Phil Owens, one of my first cousins, played for them on the wing. We were very close to his immediate family and it was I, not so long ago, who taught his father Les to drive. And, yes, he passed his test first time!

Pool is another game that I really enjoy. There was a pool table at the club in Mynyddcerrig, and since my father was a member of the committee, he would have to take his turn to clean the building. This would usually happen on a Saturday morning. From an early age, I would go to help out. But the big attraction for me at that time was being able to have a few games of pool with my father while we were there. Strictly speaking, I was too young to play according to club rules. Therefore, when I accidentally ripped the cloth on the table when attempting an ambitious trick shot, my father, fair play to him, took the blame and said that he was responsible for the damage. I remember him coming home from the next committee meeting feeling rather embarrassed because one of the other members, Cecil Jones, had told him that he was now too old to play trick shots on the pool table and that he should leave such activities to the younger members. Little did Cecil know... until now!

Cecil was one of the characters at Mynyddcerrig club. I remember watching the Six Nations there once when Stephen Jones had missed a few kicks in the Wales v France match. It was the first time BBC had introduced the arrow on the screen showing the distance and angle of the kick. After missing three consecutive kicks Cecil shouted out, 'For christ sake Stephen mun, you only have to follow the arrow!'

However, all those hours of practice paid dividends for me, because at the age of fourteen I became the Club Pool Champion. I played a lot when I was a teenager, mainly in the Mynyddcerrig club or down at the Prince pub in Porthyrhyd with friends from the Young Farmers Club, but I rarely have an opportunity to do so these days.

I became a pupil at Maes yr Yrfa school by accident. After I'd been at Gwendraeth Grammar School for a year, parents had to make a choice between sending their children there or to Maes yr Yrfa, since only comprehensive education would be available in the area from then on. The only difference between the two schools was that Maes yr Yrfa would henceforth offer education through the medium of Welsh. Yet some parents mistakenly thought that Gwendraeth was still a grammar school of sorts. It was mainly for that reason, in my opinion, that many of the pupils wanted to remain at Gwendraeth, myself included, until the very last minute. In time the position was reversed, with the majority of the area's pupils today choosing to go to Maes yr Yrfa.

My main reason for eventually wanting to leave Gwendraeth was that I was being continually bullied by a pupil in the same year as me. It got so bad at times that I didn't want to go to school at all and I often pretended that I was ill so that I could stay at home instead. When I left the house in the morning my Mum would always say, 'Have a good day and see you tonight.'

I'd say under my breath, 'Ok, see you tonight if I'm still alive.' For that period of a few months I hated school and would do anything to try and avoid going there. However, when I had to go to school, I adopted a useful ploy in order to foil the bully. The bus that picked us up at Mynyddcerrig would arrive at school each morning at about ten past eight, but after dropping us off it would then go along another route to carry other pupils to the school. So, instead of getting off with the rest of the Mynyddcerrig pupils, I would hide at the back of the bus while it went on its next journey. My friend Wayne Thomas was part of that second batch of pupils who arrived at about five minutes to nine, so I was then able to join him and benefit from his protective company before school began.

On reflection I regret very much that I didn't confide in anyone during this very painful time in my life. But telling someone else that you are being bullied is extremely difficult because you are too ashamed and embarrassed to admit it – as if you, and not the bully, were the guilty party. As it happens I am now an ambassador for the Excellence Centre Wales, which is a body, run by a great guy called Frederico, that organises workshops to help prevent bullying, particularly homophobic bullying, in schools. Therefore when I visit schools in Wales in this capacity I continually try and impress upon pupils the importance of reporting any instances of bullying.

I was fortunate in that I had a group of very good friends during that first year at secondary school and in due course they stood up to the bully, with the result that he no longer bothered me. Ever since I have hated the attitude of bullies, and when I later went to work at Maes yr Yrfa school I was always on the lookout so that I could offer assistance to anyone who suffered in that respect. The friends who rescued me from the bully at Gwendraeth had indicated that they wished to move to Maes yr Yrfa the following year. So I went with them and I've never regretted that decision, for everything that I have achieved in public life up to now is due to the positive influence of Maes yr Yrfa.

That decision had nothing to do with language or the type of education that I was going to receive. In fact, many of my lessons at Gwendraeth were given through the medium of Welsh. The school also made much of its excellent rugby tradition and was able to lay claim to such famous former pupils as Carwyn James, Barry John, Gareth Davies and Jonathan Davies. My contribution to that tradition was that I played prop for the first-year team and hated every minute of it, mainly because I was no good at all, so I didn't ever venture to play in that position after that disastrous experience. I believe that members of the front row brotherhood fully deserve any plaudits and respect which they might receive. I know, from bitter experience, that you need to be brave and strong to play there and that I have never possessed such attributes!

But from my very first day at Gwendraeth School I had a particular talent for making mischief, often at the expense of the teachers. On one occasion, before I was due to sit a biology test, I persuaded one of my friends, Paul Isaacs, that we should throw our school bags on to the roof of one of the Portakabins in the yard. We turned up for the test and informed the teacher, Eddie Biol, that someone had stolen our bags, which contained all our books and our homework, making it essential that we find them as soon as possible. So, having had the necessary permission, off we went to find Mr Owen Herbert the technology teacher, who had a ladder at his disposal, informing him that some evil pupils had thrown our bags on to the roof of the Portakabin. He managed to retrieve them safely whilst complaining, during his ascent, that he knew full well what we were up to! But the all-important factor for us was that we succeeded in missing the biology test.

On another occasion I was sent out from the art class, taught by Mrs Gaynor Hughes, for swearing and was told to go and see Elsbeth Jones, head of the Welsh department, whose class was next door. She was a very formidable lady and as pupils we were frightened to death of her. Indeed, even when I was on the staff at Maes yr Yrfa she would make me jump! However, she was a good teacher with whom you could also have a laugh and share a joke. She was actually in the middle of a lesson when I was sent to see her that day, and when I walked in she asked me what I was doing there.

'I've been sent to see you because I swore, Miss,' I answered.

'What did you say?' she asked.

'F***ing hell, Miss!'

Of course her class burst out laughing and I was sent to stand in the book cupboard at the back of the room. When I got inside, Paul Isaacs (again!) was already there, having committed some punishable offence a little earlier. But I wasn't there long because I have a phobia about being enclosed in confined spaces. So I started banging on the cupboard door, shouting for all to hear, 'Miss, you've got to let me out because I'm *claustrapheebic*.'

Once again the class burst out laughing, along with Elsbeth Jones, but at least I was set free. Unfortunately it took a long time for my mates to stop teasing me about my claustrophobia. It was no surprise perhaps to hear that Eddie Biol walked into the staff room one day and threw a pile of exercise books into the air, whilst shouting gleefully, 'Thank God! Nigel Owens and Paul Isaacs are leaving to go to Maes yr Yrfa school!'

But my mischievous ways continued in Maes yr Yrfa. One day, Jones Maths was taking registration. Whenever pupils were asked a question by him, he always wanted them to add the word 'sir' to the answer. He expected the same response during registration, but when it was my turn to reply to his 'Next!' I shouted, 'Nigel Owens!' Mr Jones said, 'Pardon?' 'Nigel Owens!' I exclaimed again. 'Are you not going to include the "sir", then?' was his response. I said, 'OK – Sir Nigel Owens!'

Another example of our wicked ways was our practice of

hiding under the Portakabins in the schoolyard during the lunch break when Mrs Ann Jones, or 'Annie Chem', an attractive red-head, walked past on her way home for lunch or back to school. As she went by we would shout out another nickname we had for her, namely 'Annie Fanny!' This was much to her embarrassment and she quickened her pace as her face went as red as her hair. Some years later when I joined her on the school staff at Maes yr Yrfa I confessed to my involvement in those incidents. She burst out laughing when she heard – and turned bright red again!

In a way I was fortunate that this comic urge didn't get me into more trouble with the staff. Thankfully they appreciated that no malice was intended and they were usually prepared to see the funny side. I must confess, however, that I went too far on one occasion. We were having a debate in an English lesson, which was being taught by Miss Williams, on fox hunting. I was speaking in favour, my friend Caroline Shirley was speaking against and one of my best mates, Craig Bonnell, was chairing the debate. Colin Price and I arrived late and, having forgotten that we were having a different kind of lesson, I asked Craig, who was sitting in the teacher's chair, 'Oh, where's the old cow then, hasn't she arrived yet?' Part of the class went very quiet and the remainder burst out laughing. Then from amongst the pupils in the middle of the room, where she was seated to mark our debating skills, came Miss Wilkins' voice, 'Yes, Mr Owens, I am here waiting for you!' She was a lovely lady but I didn't get a chance to apologise for she sent me out of the class and told me to report to the deputy head, Miss Margaret Davies, who was also a very nice lady. Since that day I have learned to look around before opening my mouth!

Of course with all this clowning I didn't give my school work anything like the attention that was required. I had some idea of becoming a vet in due course, but I was informed by one of the teachers, 'You'll never make it, you don't work hard enough.' However, there was one discipline which I really enjoyed and that was drama. I'm grateful to one teacher in particular, Delyth Mai Nicholas, for instilling in me a keen interest in that subject and for giving me a chance to appear on the stage quite often. When I was thirteen, a television producer by the name of Pat Griffiths came to the school to search for budding actors who would be required to dub the voices of characters in an Italian drama series into Welsh. I didn't know at the time that one of my father's duties when he worked at the local quarry was to visit farms in the vicinity in order to warn them that they were about to set off explosive charges, and that Pat's parents lived on one of those farms. I was fortunate to be chosen (the only one from our school, as it happened) for the series in question. I was to play the part of Pepino, a small, fat boy who was continually eating something. One of the perks of the job, for the sake of authenticity, was that I could eat lollipops and sweets all day long, even during 'takes'. I really enjoyed the experience and it no doubt instilled an even greater desire in me to perform. On top of which I was getting paid! My mother, bless her, would put that money in some kind of savings account for me, as she did with any other income I got from various sources. After many years, when I needed money for a particular purpose, a tidy little sum would become available from that account. That's how I was able, as a seventeen-year-old, to buy my first car, which was a yellow Honda Civic – Jimmy Tegfan's old car.

Travelling in the company of my parents to the big city of Cardiff for four or five dubbing sessions over a period of a few months was quite an adventure. My father didn't like driving to any place where he would have to contend with roundabouts or roads which had busy lanes of traffic, so we would travel to Cardiff by train. The dubbing schedule usually allowed me a few free hours around midday which enabled us to visit some of the city's attractions, such as the National Museum and the Arms Park, of course. When we were there, the groundsman, who was busy cutting the grass, allowed us to walk on the hallowed turf, which was a huge thrill for me at the time. I remember saying some three years later that I wouldn't go back there until I had cause to referee a game at the ground. However, I had to forget about that promise because it was decided during the 1990s that the old Arms Park would be demolished to make room for a new stadium which would be built in readiness for the 1999 Rugby World Cup, to be hosted by Wales. That new stadium is, of course, the Millennium Stadium – the greatest rugby ground in the world in my opinion, and in the opinion of numerous other rugby enthusiasts. So, in 1995, I had to return with some friends to see Wales play their last game at the Arms Park, which was against England.

CHAPTER 2

Schooldays

THE INCLINATION TO BE mischievous and the urge to be a comedian are basically very similar. There is no doubt that the person responsible for instilling the latter in me was a comedian called Ifan Gruffydd, who performs regularly on Welsh language television. As a family we always went out on a Friday evening, which was when Ifan usually appeared in his own TV series. However, I always made a point of recording his programme and watching it as soon as I came home. I then used to make sure that I had memorised all his jokes in order that I could entertain all my friends in the school cloakroom the following Monday morning. I also made an effort to mimic Ifan as closely as possible, with the result that my audience was usually quite amused by my efforts.

When I was fourteen I had my first opportunity to do a half-hour spot of comedy at the Mynyddcerrig Working Men's Club, because the entertainers who had been booked hadn't turned up. During my act I impersonated a character called Idwal, whom Ifan Gruffydd had popularised in his shows. It went down very well and that was the very first time that I felt the thrill of making an audience laugh. Indeed, that particular experience served as a significant impetus for my future endeavours as a comedian. But I also learned a very important lesson on that occasion, by making the mistake of returning to the stage later on in the evening. The response by then wasn't so good and it made me realise, even at that very early stage in my career, the importance of leaving the audience wanting more, rather than succumbing to the temptation of stretching my material to its limits!

The Young Farmers movement played a prominent part in promoting my 'public' appearances. I joined a branch in the village of Llanarthne, some six miles away, where the club leader was a local farmer called Howard Roberts. I became great friends with Howard and spent many happy years working on his farm, Y Wern, in the village of Drefach. The club operated a system whereby members from surrounding villages would be picked up by minibus every Tuesday evening, at a cost of £1 per head, and transported to Llanarthne. Such a convenient arrangement meant that I and one or two others from my area were able to attend the club on a regular basis. I made many good friends there and it's possible that my life would have been very different were it not for the Young Farmers movement. It presented me with so many opportunities to appear, in public, in such a variety of activities. For example, I enjoyed competing in the Young Farmers National Eisteddfod, particularly in categories which called for sketches and humour. I won the humorous recitation competition a few times and also had success in the joke-telling competition on one occasion, as well as taking the prize for the best performer in a thirty-minute entertainment slot. I even competed once in the hymn-singing category, but only because no one else in our club was willing to do so. I also took first prize in the public speaking competition, in Welsh and in English, on more than one occasion. That particular talent must be in the blood for my cousin Helen was also a winner several times.

Along with a few members of the Llanarthne club I was also one of a party, called Lliwiau'r Enfys, which regularly held concerts in local villages. As well as deriving great pleasure from performing with the group, I really enjoyed the fun we used to have when coming together beforehand to organise such events, when the welcome provided by Luther Rees and the family at Blaenhirwaun, and by Howard at Y Wern, was indeed memorable. All in all, these activities gave me an excellent base from which I was able, ultimately, to develop and to perform in variety concerts on stage and on television.

When it was time for me to sit my GCSE examinations, it was my intention to return to school the following year to study for A levels in drama and history. But despite passing those two subjects, my other results were disappointing. So I went back to school the following autumn with a view to re-sitting the subjects I'd failed. However, the headmaster, Arwyn Thomas, jokingly remarked one day that the school would probably have to close for some time the following week since Cliff, the caretaker, would be going into hospital. In fact they were unable to find anyone to take his place for the next eight months while he recovered from surgery, so I offered to step in. With tongue in cheek I claimed that it didn't seem such a difficult job and that I would have no problem in coping with it.

The following morning, the headmaster confirmed that the required permission had been obtained from the local education office and that the job was mine. For about a month I was both a pupil and caretaker, before deciding that the latter had the greater appeal. After all, it was just a part-time job which entailed going in at 6.30 in the morning to light the boilers and get the school ready for the day to come. I would knock off at 9.30am and then return from 3.30 to 6.30pm. For this I was paid £120 a week, but I didn't laze about and put my feet up during the hours I was away from the school – I would work on Y Wern farm. I used to love spending time there, regardless of whether I had work to do or not, for Howard, his wife Margaret, his mother Mrs Roberts, and the children Nia and Neville, always made me feel like one of the family and the farm became my second home. I still call there from time to time but not as often as I would like.

A caretaker's work is important to every school, and I hasten to add that by that time I was considerably more mature. I had shown in various ways that I was now a person who could assume responsibility. In the past I had organised the school shop every morning, I'd acted in quite a few school productions and had done many 'spots' as an impersonator in concerts – the favourites being Ifan Gruffydd and a few of the teachers. By this time I'd also begun to referee. Apparently, one of the teachers would use my name as an example of a once-wicked boy who became courteous and likeable, yet who was still prone to harmless mischief. In other words I would now make the teachers laugh whereas previously I made them mad!

I was, of course, initially very inexperienced as a caretaker. My first duty of the day, as I have mentioned, was to light the boilers so that the school, and the kitchen in particular, would have heat and hot water. In order to do this, the fire had to be stoked the previous night so that it remained alight in the morning. However, on my very first day in the job I realised that I had forgotten to do this, with the result that I had to telephone my father at 6.30am after he'd just arrived home from working the night shift at the quarry. He had to rush down to the school with a stock of firewood so that I could light the boilers. Without his assistance that morning the school would have had to close for the day and my reputation as a caretaker would have been in tatters before I'd even started in the job.

It was difficult to keep a balance between being on good terms with members of the staff and maintaining my friendships with many of the pupils, particularly those with whom I continued to socialise in the Young Farmers Club. Fortunately, many of the more mischievous amongst them had left school by that time. Yet the old urge to play a trick or two was still there. For example, I was persuaded by some of the lads in the sixth form to lock one of the most attractive lady teachers in her room where she was marking books after school, so that we could all gawp at her climbing out through the window when it was time for her to leave.

I enjoyed my time as caretaker and, probably because I was so young, the seven lady cleaners at the school looked after me as if I was their son. I also took great delight in teasing them at every opportunity, but the high point of the week was our informal gathering for tea and biscuits at the end of every Friday afternoon. From the time I began to impersonate Idwal in public, they insisted that I dress in my 'Idwal' clothes and regale them with my repertoire of his jokes. However, they must have cursed me on occasions when they became the butt of my practical jokes, such as locking them inside whatever room they happened to be cleaning or removing the plug from its socket when they were using the Hoover, perhaps some distance away, then taking great delight in secretly watching them as they tried to discover why it had stopped working. Not all my pranks were so innocent. It was the cleaners' practice at the end of the day to bang their large woollen brushes against a brick wall near the boiler house, in order to get rid of all the dust and fluff they had picked up. One day I hid in the boiler house and as they all lined up for the brush cleaning, I turned the hose on them. They were drenched, and as they ran for cover in total panic I'm sure their screams could be heard in the next village.

I was aware that once he had fully recovered Cliff intended to return to his caretaker duties for a year, before taking retirement. It was my hope that I could then be appointed as permanent caretaker in his place, and it appeared that the school was happy with that arrangement. So I spent that year working full-time as a farm hand at Y Wern and, since I had formally registered under the YTS job scheme, I got paid for working there. In accordance with that particular programme I would also spend a few days each week at the Pibwrlwyd and Gelli Aur training farms, where we would be taught such varied subjects as how to protect the countryside, hedging practices, fencing techniques, milking methods and so on. My personal interests there were generally to do with husbandry but it was also a period of great enjoyment in the company of many good friends. If I were totally honest, I would say that my main reason for attending the college each Friday was to meet up with friends, like Arwel Cottage, Gethin, Aled Mawr, Simon Penclun, Ryan and Andrew Clarke. In my first term there, one of my favourite pastimes was having regular car races with Simon along Pibwrlwyd Flats, we being the only two members of the gang who could drive at that time. My driving, however, wasn't always to be commended. Once, when driving in Carmarthen, I cut up one of my lecturers at a roundabout. She was not amused and, quite rightly, tore a strip off me during the following week's lecture.

I took a lot of pleasure from socialising, as it were, with the Young Farmers set. Some were older than me and I got into trouble on more than one occasion by trying to prove to myself that I was just as experienced as they were, particularly in the matter of sinking pints of beer. I recall going to Carmarthen with them one Saturday and, although I tried to keep up with their drinking exploits, by 11.30pm I knew that I'd had enough. So I looked for a taxi and asked the driver to take me home to Mynyddcerrig. When the driver shouted that we were almost there, I put my hand in my pocket to find that I didn't have a cent left. My only option, it appeared to me, was to leg it from the taxi in order to avoid having to pay. So I bolted from there like a greyhound. I cleared two garden walls to the sound of the driver bellowing and cursing somewhere behind me. Unfortunately I came a cropper at the third 'fence' and went flying into a flower bed. Although I was in some pain, from what turned out to be a 'dead' leg, I lay there quite still amongst the pansies and the tulips until I heard the sound of the taxi leaving. I got to my feet and looked around in order get my bearings. It didn't take long for me to realise that the taxi had brought me to the village of Mynyddygarreg, near Cydweli, instead of Mynyddcerrig, and that I was now faced with a walk of some eight miles to get home. Since I was a little drunk and handicapped by a dead leg, that journey was particularly long and painful. That was a harsh lesson, and I vowed that from then on I would choose my drinking friends more carefully and that I would always carry enough money to get a taxi.

Every Sunday evening I would go out for a meal with friends from Pontyberem – nothing flashy, just a trip to McDonald's or somewhere similar. One Sunday we went to Ammanford for a kebab and returned late that night to the village square in Pontyberem, whereupon the old urge to create mischief raised its head once again. There were building contractors working opposite the home of two of my best friends, the brothers Wayne and Gary Thomas. They were constructing what is now the old folks' complex called Nantyglo. So Willis, Steven Davies, Matthew Rowe and I decided to have some fun by moving the contractors' Portaloo toilet onto the brothers' front lawn, where it stood in all its glory like Dr Who's Tardis. We also relocated some cones and diversion signs so that all traffic at that particular spot would end up at the front of Gary and Wayne's house. However, the Thomas family woke up as we were put the finishing touches to our masterplan so we had to beat a hasty retreat. As I drove off laughing, with the other lads hiding in the back seat, I could see Wayne sprinting after us, picking up a cone and hurling it in the direction of the car. I had only had the vehicle, a white Peugeot 205, for a few weeks, so Wayne would not have had an opportunity to see me driving it. But he telephoned Gary, who was at college in Cardiff, with a description of the car, whereupon he was told, 'Owens, bloody Owens has just bought one!' To make matters worse, Wayne and his elder brother Roger, who happened to be there at the time, were not, unfortunately, nearly as careful as we had been when they moved the portable toilet back to its original location. In their agitated state they accidentally tipped the building workers' faeces all over the lawn, which literally left a huge stink in front of their house for days and which became the village talking point for some time. Wayne has never been known for his tolerance and patience with the result that if he happens to blow a fuse, it's time to retire at speed. Somehow he got to know of our part in the Portaloo conspiracy and we had no option but to keep clear of Pontyberem Rugby Club for many weeks, until he'd had a chance to cool down.

During the daytime, I was happy enough doing the usual farming tasks at Y Wern. I was always quite busy, particularly at such times as the hay harvest when I'd be required to do a lot of baling. On one occasion I was working a small field in Pontyberem under an arrangement whereby Y Wern would have half the bales and the owners of the field, Mynachlog farm, would have the other half. (They only kept horses and consequently didn't have adequate machinery to harvest the hay themselves.) I had driven the tractor carrying the bales through the village with Phil Tynewydd, who lived on a small holding next to Y Wern and who had helped to load the trailer. He was a very friendly and funny old chap, with a dry sense of humour. He had been standing at the front of the trailer behind the tractor and had continually been passing comments such as, 'Slow down here!' or 'Drive carefully, now, because if this load falls off I shall be away like a shot and denying that I'm involved!' Sure enough, as I drove through the village square the bales tipped from the trailer and rolled all over the road. It's a very busy place, with a constant flow of traffic passing through, so my first thought was to jump down from the tractor to try and direct the various vehicles that were trying to weave their way through the bales. After a while I went around the back of the trailer to see how Phil was progressing with the job of reloading some of the bales. True to his word, as always, he was nowhere to be seen. I eventually found him in the cafe on the square enjoying a cup of tea and taking great delight from the fact that so many people were calling me all the names under the sun and that my reputation in the area as a tractor driver was ruined. I'm sure the people of Pontyberem cursed me more then than they have ever done during my career as a referee.

Even during the days when I looked after the dogs at Tir

Garn I had a special relationship with animals. At that time Dilys had a dog, Bel, which was quite ferocious and which most people approached at their peril. Yet I could do anything I wanted with her. When I was fifteen years old, Bel had a number of puppies, one of which I bought and also called Bel. I had wanted a dog of my own ever since our time at Moultan where I had a lovely dog called Queeny. My aim was to have Bel produce a few litters so I could make some money and also have a pet of my own. However, we only managed to have one litter from her, which produced two beautiful puppies. We sold them both, although I would have liked to have kept them because that was the whole point of the exercise. Unfortunately, Bel died suddenly when she was six years old, which left us devastated as a family. At the time I was employed as a technician at Maes yr Yrfa, but I wasn't able to go to work for three days after losing Bel because I was so upset.

After that my parents declared that we would never have another dog, since the trauma of losing Bel had been too great. But a year or so later I decided to buy a West Highland Terrier pup, just like Bel, as a Christmas present for my parents. On that Christmas Eve I went to pick up the dog from Cwm Hywel farm in Llannon, a neighbouring village. After calling on my grandmother in Drefach in to order to show her the intended gift, I took the pup home and hid it in the shed with a view to introducing it to my parents the following morning. But the little blighter started to kick up a racket in the shed and my father soon found her. As a result there was an almighty row during which my parents read me the riot act. The upshot was that I had to take the dog back to Cwm Hywel that night. My grandmother and Ken had joined us for Christmas lunch, as they had done for many years, but I did nothing throughout the meal but begrudge the fact that the little dog had been so badly treated. It was undoubtedly the saddest Christmas Day that I had ever experienced up until then, but I had learned an important lesson: namely that it was unwise to make any arrangements which concerned our household unless my parents' permission had been obtained in advance.

One day the vet came to Y Wern to put one of the dogs, Sheba, to sleep because she was very sick. It had also been decided to put down Lassie, another of the farm dogs, because she was now too old to work. However, I was very fond of Lassie and shortly before the vet was due I took her up to the mountain nearby and tethered her where she couldn't be seen from the farm. When the vet arrived, Lassie was nowhere to be seen, despite the fact that her name was called continuously. Late that afternoon I went to get her from the mountain. As we approached the farm I took off her tether, after which she trotted nonchalantly into the yard to everyone's amazement.

As a result of that little adventure, Howard believed that the way Lassie had sensed the vet's arrival to put her down had been uncanny (!) so he decided that she could spend the rest of her days on Y Wern, where she lived for a further three years. Yet my favourite dog there was Rex; wherever I went, so did he. If I was out working on the fields he would always be running in front of the tractor with the result that, after a while, I would open the tractor door and he would jump up and sit beside me. Perhaps an indication of my regard for the farm animals was the fact that every so often I would choose not to eat bacon there, even though it was something I really enjoyed. The reason for this was that Howard and Margaret reared pigs to be slaughtered and eaten. It was usually my job to feed them with swill and the left-overs from milking. I'd become so attached to them that I could never think of eating them. I remember taking some pigs to the Pwll Bach slaughter house in Felinfoel. I couldn't bear to see and hear them being killed, despite the alleged painless and humane methods that were used. I never went to the slaughter house again.

Mrs Roberts (Howard's mother) was a real character and I used to have a lot of fun with her. She once bought a new Hoover from a travelling salesman who would call by the farm every so often, offering various bargains. Mrs Roberts was a shrewd customer who was always on the look-out for a good deal and she was looking forward enthusiastically to giving the house a complete going over with her new Hoover. As I cycled to work that morning, I stopped at a telephone kiosk in Drefach, a few hundred yards from Y Wern, to call Mrs Roberts, pretending that I was a policeman from the local station in Cross Hands. I told her, in a posh voice, that I had been informed that she had bought the Hoover from a person whom the police were investigating on suspicion of selling stolen goods and that I would have to come and collect the appliance. Her response, after initially letting rip with a few curses, was, 'You can come if you like, but you'll have to wait for me to finish Hoovering the house before you can take the machine away!' She had quite a shock, yet was very relieved when the 'policeman' arrived. He, nevertheless, had to suffer even more abuse when all was revealed!

Although I enjoyed farming, I paid little attention to the educational aspects of agriculture at Pibyrlwyd and Gelli Aur since I knew that I would probably be resuming my duties as a school caretaker at the beginning of the following school year. However, that's not what actually happened. Howard Y Wern used to do a lot of contracting work on local farms which included hedge-cutting. It was a job that, if it was to be done well, required a degree of patience and much skill. As it happened, I began to get a reputation as someone who was quite good at it, so I was often called upon. Ieuan Morgan, the head of science at Maes yr Yrfa, had asked me to cut the hedges at Stafell, his smallholding in the village of Llanddarog. He must have been pleased with the standard and perhaps realised that I was quite adept at manual work. Consequently I was asked if I would like to have a job at Maes yr Yrfa as a technician, working in the science laboratories and in the technology department. I would also be in charge of the resources and photocopying departments. This offer came just at the right time, for my YTS programme and period of employment at Y Wern were due to end in a few months. Since it was only a small dairy farm milking around 50 or 60 cows, it would not have been possible to employ a full-time worker there without the assistance of a scheme such as that offered by the YTS. Work as a technician was certainly more interesting than being a caretaker and the pay was definitely better!

That was a very happy time in my life and had I not been attracted to refereeing it's possible that I would still be doing that work in Maes yr Yrfa. Everyone, staff and pupils alike, addressed me as 'Nigel' and I got on well with almost everybody. I had so much fun while working there particularly with colleagues in the science laboratories 'prep' room, such as Bill, Caryl, and later Sharon. One person in particular, Robert Samms, the caretaker, was great company and he shared with me an inclination to make mischief. I also had many laughs with the girls in the office. In retrospect it could be argued that we sometimes went overboard. One day the headmaster, Arwyn Thomas, had called a staff meeting at the end of the lunch hour since it was the last day of term before the summer holidays. The tradition was to congregate in the small but cosy staff room to say our goodbyes and present gifts to those who were retiring or moving on. Robert and I had decided that it would be quite a laugh if we excused ourselves from the meeting and locked all the other staff members in the room, so that one of them would have to climb out of a window to obtain a key. However, when we overheard Dai Williams, one of the technology teachers, who was himself a bit of a character, asking the headmaster (who had been trying in vain to open the door) whether it was a coincidence that the only two members of staff who hadn't turned up for the meeting were myself and Robert, we quickly and quietly unlocked the door and bolted for the seclusion of the science labs, like two naughty schoolboys.

One pupil had been giving Robert and me a lot of hassle.

Nothing nasty, just good humoured banter and the occasional practical joke. Therefore, just before the morning assembly was about to commence one day, we grabbed the troublesome pupil, tied him to a chair and put him behind the curtains on the stage in the school hall. He was forced stay there in silence throughout the assembly since the headmaster and the pupils taking part in the service were just the other side of the curtain, with the remainder of the school seated facing the stage. Of course he was too ashamed to draw attention to his predicament or he would have been a laughing stock throughout the school for a long time. We had no problem with him after that incident but neither was there any ill feeling between us. Times have changed since then, along with society. I don't think we would be allowed to have such fun these days. There's no doubt that political correctness has gone too far.

Sometimes, however, the school staff had a chance to have some fun at my expense. I remember being sent by the headmaster and Susan Roberts, the head of finance at the school, to Leekes, the local superstore, in order to buy weights which were to be attached to the bottom of window blinds at the school. I later twigged that there were no such objects, but not before I'd spent ages searching around the store and making many enquiries. All was revealed when a large group of the store's staff gathered in front of me at the check-out to shout, 'April Fool!' I hadn't realised the significance of the date. I couldn't believe that I had fallen for it, especially since I had caught out so many friends and colleagues in the past with similar pranks.

A technician's job can be quite dangerous at times, particularly when handling certain chemicals or electrical equipment. I was twice taken to get medical attention, but only because of my own carelessness and stupidity. The first time was when I was preparing equipment on the circular saw for a technology project while simultaneously talking to Neville, the son at Y Wern farm. My hand slipped against the blade and

43

suddenly there was blood everywhere, at which point I almost passed out. I was taken to the local surgery to have the wound stitched, but the greatest pain I suffered was the relentless leg-pulling that I had to face at the school for weeks afterwards.

Another time, Robert Samms was on his knees in one of the corridors trying to repair a bolt at the foot of a door. I came up quietly behind him and decided to give him a bit of a shock by leapfrogging over him. Unfortunately, as I sailed through the air, I hit my head on the upper frame of the door. Robert had to take me at once to Glangwili Hospital in Carmarthen, where I had eight stitches inserted in my head wound. Because so many people needed medical attention that day, we didn't get back to school until 7.30pm. As a result, Iwan Rees, the headmaster at that time, had to stay behind to await our return, since Robert was the only person who had a key to lock the school. Iwan was not a happy man that night!

A technician's job didn't pay all that well, so I would moonlight a little by taking on some evening work in the area. For a year or two I helped out with a milk round on two or three evenings a week and I became great friends with the owners of the business, Eirian and Linda, and the boys, Michael and Kevin, spending many happy hours with the family. For about four years after that, along with Tracy Roberts and Alana Davies, I helped to run a number of local youth clubs held in various villages in the vicinity. This work was done under the direction of Menter Cwm Gwendraeth (the Gwendraeth Valley Venture) which is a body set up expressly to promote the use of the Welsh language in the area. I was involved every weekday evening and I really enjoyed the experience. Apart from the youth clubs, young people in the local villages had very few amenities at their disposal, so it's more than likely they would otherwise have been out and about and up to no good. What was rewarding for me was that so many of them seemed to really appreciate what we offered. It wasn't just a case of arranging trips and activities such as table tennis, pool, darts, PlayStation, and card and board games; we also organised educational sessions such as drug, alcohol and smoking abuse workshops and anti-bullying, birth control, first aid and self-defence classes, undertaken by qualified people in those fields.

We also arranged regular social excursions such as ice-skating in Cardiff, biking trips and visits to the Oakwood Leisure Park in Pembrokeshire. One of our more regular trips was to Swansea, to the cinema or the ten-pin bowling or Lazer Dome. We would have as many as 150 members going with us and, in order to facilitate transport arrangements, I took a driving course with Carmarthenshire Council which allowed me to take youth club members in the minibus.

One Thursday evening, I took Pontyberem youth club to Swansea along with Alana, for some bowling and a cinema visit. A member who never missed the club evenings was Rhodri Tudor. He was sixteen years old and, despite suffering from cerebral palsy and having to receive 24-hour care, he was always smiling, pleasant, polite and a central part of everything we did as a club. It really was a pleasure to have him in our company. We would usually call in at McDonald's on the way home, and on this particular night we stopped at the one in Cross Hands. As usual I got Rhodri's wheelchair out of the bus and put his cushion, which he was very fussy about, in its customary position. Then I lifted him out of the bus and put him in the chair. Having done so, I was so concerned with making sure I had locked the bus properly that I had forgotten to engage the handbrake on Rhodri's wheelchair. I suddenly heard him shouting, 'Nige! Nige!' By the time I realised what was happening, Rhodri was speeding across the car park, laughing heartily as he went. He fortunately came to an abrupt halt when the chair struck the front of a parked car, but by that time my heart was in my mouth. Thankfully no harm came to anyone and Rhodri thought it was the most hilarious incident that had ever happened to him. It certainly taught me a lesson concerning the importance of securing the handbrake at all times.

Although the emphasis in the youth club was on enjoyment, it also gave me an opportunity to provide a few other services. For example, perhaps as a result of my own experiences, I feel very strongly about bullying. If someone, perhaps a friend or parent, drew my attention to the fact that one of the club members was being bullied, I would then be able to do something about it – usually by having a quiet word with the person responsible. I had an advantage by virtue of the fact that I knew the vast majority of the members and they knew me, since they were also pupils at Maes yr Yrfa. The relationship I had with them was, of course, much more informal than that which existed between them and members of the teaching staff. So when a problem occurred, they would feel much more comfortable talking about it with me in the relaxed atmosphere of the club. There were many instances when parents came to thank me specifically for dealing with certain matters which had been preying on the minds of some of these young people.

My youth club activities gave me so much pleasure that I went on a course for prospective youth workers, and it's possible that I would now be working in that field if I hadn't become a professional referee. In fact, although I haven't yet decided what I want to do with my life when my refereeing days have ended, I will give serious consideration to going back to working with young people.

CHAPTER 3

The Entertainer

AT THE END OF the 1980s I was getting more and more work as a comedian. I had started as a barman in the Prince of Wales pub in Porthyrhyd along with John, Heulwen and their daughter Leslie. Saturday night was always very busy and people came from far and wide to hear the locals sing and to join in themselves. There were many characters there but the star turn was John, the landlord, who had a magnificent voice, with Gom providing accompaniment on the organ. They were usually ably assisted by other regulars such as Ken Lewis, father of Emyr Lewis, the former rugby international, and John Greville from Porthyrhyd. In order to add a little variety to the proceedings I would sometimes leave the bar to tell a few jokes, which seemed to be well received. So much so that I was eventually expected to do a spot every Saturday night, particularly when there was a party or when a coach trip had stopped for some bar snacks. I used to love telling jokes at the Prince for it was a place where I could get away with material I couldn't use at other venues where I was getting invitations to perform, such as Young Farmers clubs and social occasions in local chapels and village halls.

One of the traditional forms of Welsh entertainment is a variety concert called *noson lawen*, which can be translated as 'an evening of light entertainment'. One of the key participants in these events is the compere, and in due course I was being asked to compere events as well as doing a comic spot. After performing at one such event at Llandovery Rugby Club, two members of a band, Charlie and Gari, recommended me to a television producer, Hefin Elis, with whom they often worked. He was responsible at the time for a TV show called *Noson Lawen* and I was subsequently invited to take part in a programme which was being televised from Abergelli Fach farm, Felindre, near Morriston. I appeared as a character I had invented for that particular programme, called Mostyn. I came on to the stage dressed in a long brown coat and a large, funny tartan hat, riding an old bike, which I had borrowed from the late Will Page, a neighbour in Mynyddcerrig. It was a big occasion for me, with many stars of the Welsh variety scene, such as Gillian Elisa, John and Alun and my boyhood hero, Ifan Gruffydd, appearing on the bill. Although I was very nervous, I was determined to do well and I got a favourable response from the audience. My co-artists, who had been very supportive during the day, were also very complementary. I must have done alright that night, for Hefin asked me the following year if I would like to compere the programme every so often, which I did for the first time on a show that was televised from Godor farm, Nantgaredig, in 1992. I really thought and felt that I had hit the big time.

Unfortunately *Noson Lawen*, on which I appeared for some fifteen years, has now finished. We would arrive at each programme's location at about four o'clock, which would leave us a few hours to prepare and rehearse before recording. During this time I would sit down with the producer, usually Olwen Meredydd, to give her an idea of the jokes that I planned to tell. Although each spot in the actual televised programme would usually contain just two jokes, I would always tell three or four in the recording. Despite the fact that Olwen would ask me for clean jokes I would normally include a cross-section of ones which were clean, funny and near to the knuckle, so that the producer could choose, when editing the programme, the jokes which had drawn the best response from the audience during the recording. Another of Olwen's reasons for wanting to hear the jokes was because she was afraid that I would include some which, although funny, would perhaps be too blue. In that connection I must confess that there were times when I chose not to let Olwen hear some of the jokes until I was actually on stage since I knew that the blue jokes often got the best reaction from the audience!

It wasn't easy finding material as a compere for *Noson Lawen*. I had to make sure that I had a new batch of funny stories for each programme I fronted, which every other compere also had to do of course. For, once I'd told a particular joke on television, it wouldn't be possible to use it again. Well, not for a few years anyway. In the beginning the only way I had of remembering whether I'd told a joke on a previous occasion was by scrolling through video tapes of programmes that had been televised. Later, however, I began writing down when exactly I had told each joke and at what location, so that I wouldn't be guilty of repetition.

The type of humour that appeals to me is the traditional stand-up comic material of comedians such as Ken Goodwin, Ken Dodd and Bernard Manning. There are also comedians from the modern era whom I like, such as Alan Carr, Peter Kay and Lee Evans. I have no regard for what is referred to as 'alternative comedy' but I am a big fan of traditional situation comedy and I love series such as *Only Fools and Horses* and especially *High Hopes*. I am also a big fan of *Little Britain*, although, as in many other television programmes, the gay characters tend to be stereotypes. I do, however, see the funny side of 'Dafydd, the only gay in the village' and it's great to see that the world hasn't always got to be politically correct and that we can still laugh and joke about each other. As it happens, I think Wales has some of the best comedians around at the moment, for example, Colin Price. I am often the guest speaker at functions which also include the likes of Colin as comedians, so I always insist on doing my bit before they take the stage, for having to follow them would be asking for trouble.

I have always tried to make sure that I have an extensive

repertoire of jokes to draw upon. I would have heard most of them as I went about my daily routine, on Y Wern farm, in the Prince of Wales, in the Mynyddcerrig Working Men's Club, in the Young Farmers movement and while meeting with some of the village characters. One of them, Bernard Dix, had moved to the village and had become a prominent member of the community. He'd made a special effort to learn Welsh and it's a pity that more of the non-Welsh speakers who'd settled in the area didn't follow his example, although we've been very lucky in Mynyddcerrig in that most of the people who've moved into the community have made a sepcial effort to be part of it.

A great character whose company I enjoyed in the Prince was Mel 'Bach', a retired farmer. His witty quips were legendary and many a customer dreaded being the butt of his leg-pulling. I was usually spared that embarrassment, perhaps because he depended on me for a lift home from the pub, despite the fact that he lived just 75 yards away! However, the first time I met him, I was also the subject of one of his tongue-lashings. During a game of pool, I left the table to go to the toilet and accidentally left the bar-room door open. Mel usually sat by the door and that night it was bitterly cold outside, so he had to get up to close it. On my way back I inadvertently left the door open again, before resuming the game. 'Oi!' Mel shouted in my direction, in a voice that was obviously affected by a very bad chest. 'What's the matter?' I replied. 'You see this f****** frame here?' he asked. 'Well the door fits in it!' That comment really tickled me and brought the house down, as it were, and we became great friends from then on. I also valued the company of many of the Prince's other characters such as Arthur and Wally Brynlluan, all of whom have now unfortunately have passed away.

Another source of good jokes in those days was the Berem Drama Company. As a member I derived great pleasure from taking part in its productions throughout the local area and from socialising with a number of great characters such as

Gwilym Sid Davies. He would always be telling me jokes which I could use in my routines and was a great help. When I was just sixteen, I asked a number of local entertainers, who were accustomed to telling jokes on stage, whether they would be willing to help me prepare for my first appearance on television by letting me 'borrow' some of their stories, but they weren't all that happy to oblige. In view of the difficulties I faced at first in trying to get hold of comic material, I always try my best these days to help any budding comedian who asks me whether I have a joke or two they could use.

Another outlet for some of my jokes has been the many 'best man' speeches that I have been asked to write for friends' weddings, although I haven't yet appeared in that particular role myself. I was once invited by a good pal of mine, Huw Watkins, and Yvette, his wife by now, to be his best man, but he was getting married in Australia at a time when I was refereeing in South Africa.

I always tried my jokes out on my parents first, even if some tended to be a little racy. They wouldn't laugh at some jokes although I knew that they were funny. I would then try to take comfort from the fact that it was always easier to get laughs when people came together as an audience. However, if one of my jokes fell on stony ground at home, I would impress upon my parents not to come to the recording at which I intended to tell it. Yet my mother would always turn up, travelling on the coach which she would have arranged herself for the locals and family to come and support me. My father came to my first show at Abergelli Fach farm, as did my grandmother. She was also present at my second televised programme at Godor farm in Nantgaredig and I was so pleased to see her, during transmission a few weeks later, apparently having a great time. I'm so glad she was able to be part of it as not long after she passed away.

I have to say that appearing before the audiences of *Noson Lawen*, usually in an adapted barn, gave me a great deal of pleasure. I always felt comfortable standing before a gathering of country characters who were intent on having a good time. Yet there are certain other performances which stand out. I remember being given a rousing standing ovation by an audience of 250 people following my spot at a *noson lawen* in the village of Meincie. It was the first (and last!) time that I experienced such a response.

Some occasions are memorable for the wrong reasons. It was sometimes difficult to get an audience to respond and I had to be on my toes to get them to laugh. At the start of a bilingual concert in Glanaman, all my jokes seemed to be falling on deaf ears. I was the compere and responsible for the warm-up; that is, for getting the audience into a 'laughing' mood – well, that's what was supposed to happen. There was one chap, dressed in a rather gaudy light-coloured suit, yellow shirt and orange tie, who was intent on trying to wind me up, shouting comments such as, 'Come on then, make us laugh!' which I found quite disconcerting. Eventually I turned towards him and asked, 'Do you really want me to make this audience laugh? All right, let me borrow your suit!' Everybody laughed and the evening got better from then on. Top of the bill that night was Bobby Wayne, a kind and talented man who came to my assistance when the audience made things difficult for me at the outset.

A stand-up comic is sometimes faced with the problem of realising, when he is halfway through telling a joke, that he shouldn't have started it in the first place. Fortunately this has only happened to me once and I was lucky enough not to have egg on my face as a result. I hate people who are racially prejudiced, but when I told a joke about a young coloured pupil whom I claimed attended Mynyddcerrig school, I thought the audience would appreciate it for what it was – namely, a funny little story about the innocent humour displayed by small children.

This was the joke. The little coloured lad in question was very bright and, although popular with the other children, he sometimes got on their nerves a little. One day the teacher told the class, 'I am now going to give you a quiz, and I shall be giving £1 for every correct answer I get from you. Here's the first question: Which politician said, 'Give us the tools and we'll finish the job!'?' The coloured pupil immediately replied, 'Winston Churchill, in 1942, Miss.' 'Very good,' replied the teacher, 'here's your £1!' One of the other children whispered loudly, 'Pity that little black blighter didn't go home!' 'Who said that?' exclaimed the teacher. 'Enoch Powell, in 1968, Miss,' was the answer she got from one of the class.

My problem was that about half a minute into the joke, I noticed a coloured man in the audience and I became a little concerned. Fortunately, however, I could see he was laughing as I told the joke and that was my saving grace. I could have found myself in a very embarrassing situation.

However, I was embarrassed on another occasion. One of the greatest honours that has come my way in the rugby world was when I was asked to officially open the new clubhouse at Machynlleth and to be the guest of honour at the function that would be held to mark the occasion. I had by that time already opened a few summer and Christmas fetes but not a rugby club or similar establishment. At the appointed time I was asked to pull back a curtain to reveal a plaque stating that the Machynlleth RFC clubhouse had been opened by Nigel Owens in August 2008. I felt so proud at that moment and will always be grateful to the club for bestowing such an honour upon me. Following the unveiling of the plaque I gave an address which naturally included a few jokes. I often like to start such a spot by pretending to have a message which I had been asked to read out by the barman, such as, 'Has anyone here got a black Escort?' This invariably leads to someone saying, 'Yes, I have.' To which I reply, 'Oh! Well, can you go and help her? She's locked herself in the toilet!' This usually gets a great response but on this occasion the joke went down even better, and the audience kept laughing louder and louder. I knew something was up, and when I looked around I saw a lovely young black girl working behind the bar. At that point I hoped the floor would open up and swallow me. I felt really embarrassed, but I was saved by the good-humoured way the barmaid responded. I gave her a wave and said, 'Oops, I'm sorry! I didn't see you there!' To which she replied, 'It's OK, love. I know I'm black but I'm no escort, mind!'

My joke-telling exploits were not confined to local concerts and *Noson Lawen*. I appeared regularly on a Welsh-language television series on S4C called *Jocars*, which corresponded to *The Comedians*, formerly a popular series on UK television. Those responsible for *Jocars* were the late Elwyn Williams (brother of the deceased singer and entertainer, Gari Williams) and Idris Charles. I really enjoyed that experience, mainly because it gave me an opportunity to spend time with some great comics such as Don Davies (who could make people laugh without uttering a single word), Glan Davies and the late Dilwyn Davies, but also because much of the script was written for us in advance. Idris, who is a comic in his own right, would take us through it before doing an 'as live' recording in front of an audience at Theatr Felin Fach, near Aberaeron. I learned a lot about the art of stand-up in the workshops and rehearsals in Aberystwyth prior to filming, particularly the one attended by Jim Bowen, who hosted the TV programme *Bullseye* and was a former star of *The Comedians*. It was a great privilege to listen to what he had to say.

Usually I get a pretty good response from audiences. Yet some are different to others. I have only once appeared on stage in north Wales – at the Colwyn Bay Theatre in a tribute night to Dai Jones, one of the foremost Welsh language entertainers. It was a privilege to be a part of it, because if I had to choose two people who qualified for the title 'greatest Welshman', Dai would be one and Ray Gravell the other. I managed to get the audience to laugh but it wasn't one of my best nights. It was hard graft, mainly because my accent and south Wales dialect served as a kind of barrier which seemed to prevent the audience from understanding some of my jokes. Or, dare I ask, could it have been a case of north Wales humour being a little different to that to which we are accustomed in south Wales?

I returned to north Wales to present 'An Evening with Nigel Owens' at Dolgellau Rugby Club and got a fantastic response. In fact I spent a whole day there and presented some young lads with medals and trophies following a rugby tournament. It was pleasing to see that rugby at grass-roots levels in the not-so-traditional rugby areas of Wales was thriving and developing. I am firmly of the opinion that each of the four Welsh regional clubs should play at least one game a season in north Wales so that the public there can have opportunities to watch top-class rugby. There is a great deal of young rugby talent there which needs to be nurtured and supported. I know the WRU under the guidance of Roger Lewis are doing great work and is actively engaged in trying to promote the game in that part of the country, but getting the regions to play some matches there would be a great boost.

In our locality the *noson lawen* gradually died out; not because they had lost their popularity but because strict health and safety requirements made them far too difficult to arrange. By the end of the 1990s I was asked to do more spots at events which were held in rugby clubs and pubs. I decided that I would be able to expand my contribution by performing entirely on my own for an evening, offering a combination of comedy and singing. To make my work easier, I bought a sound system which enabled me to record backing tracks on a keyboard for the songs I would be performing, in the house of a relative. The relative in question was Dai Lewis, my aunt Sylvia's husband, who regularly played the keyboard in the Prince. His daughter Julie's partner at the time, Tony, who played in a local group called Side Effects and who happened to live next door to me in Mynyddcerrig would help me choose tracks which best suited my needs and adapted them if necessary to the key that would be best for me. My repertoire was quite varied, ranging from Robbie Williams numbers to songs by popular Welsh artists such as Dafydd Iwan. Later on, since I felt rather awkward when I sang with just a mike in my hand, I bought a guitar so that I could pretend to strum a few chords. It was all a sham, although there was apparently much debate as to whether I was actually playing the guitar or not.

I remember one occasion when I appeared in a concert at the Edwinsford Arms in Talley, near Llandeilo. The main act was Trebor Edwards, one of our foremost entertainers, who has a magnificent tenor voice and is always a pleasure to share a stage with. I had done my stint of telling jokes and then proceeded to sing to my usual backing tracks, whilst pretending to play the guitar. There was a group of about six people sitting at a table near the front of the stage who seemed to be paying particular attention to my hand as I strummed the guitar. I could hear comments such as, 'Yes, he's playing it, look,' and 'I'm telling you, he's not!' I got a little fed up with this, so as the backing music continued to play I took my strumming hand off the strings and stuck two fingers up at them to the rhythm of the music. Everyone in the room burst out laughing and applauded, thinking it was part of my act! To the contrary, for I had really wanted them to think that I could play the guitar. However, I swear that some day I will learn to play the guitar properly – although I wasted my chance to learn the piano as a lad. I was given lessons but I never used to practise. In the end I would refuse to turn up for the lessons even, since going out to play with my mates seemed more important to me at the time. My mother always told me that some day I would be sorry that I gave up learning to play the piano, and she was right. I have often regretted my willingness to forfeit such a great opportunity.

These days I do little work as a stand-up comic. Most of my engagements now are as an after-dinner speaker. I find that I am no longer expected to tell jokes but rather to recount my experiences both on and off the rugby field, which always seem to go down well. Every so often such events leave a lasting memory, such as the time I appeared in Tumble in front of an audience of 350 people. The function was arranged to raise money for cancer research, in memory of one of my best friends, Elsie's father, Byron Jones of Hirwaun Forge who had recently passed away quite suddenly. I got an excellent reception, but I have to confess I was extremely nervous that night, probably because I was performing in front of many friends and a local audience, which I always find more difficult to do.

A few days later I refereed the Heineken Cup semi-final match between Saracens and Munster in front of 32,000 people, but I was less nervous than that night in Tumble. In fact I rarely get nervous before refereeing a match these days, but I like to relax beforehand by listening to some music on my iPod. On the other hand, if I have a big match in the Heineken Cup, or an international, and the other officials are from Wales, the changing room is usually buzzing with banter and leg-pulling. Strangely enough, that kind of fun only seems to occur when Welsh officials are on duty. Referees and assistant referees from other countries are generally fairly quiet before games, except when characters such as Tony Spreadbury and Alan Lewis are involved. Their changing rooms are similar to ours, without being quite so noisy. But, of course, some ten minutes before kick-off, the banter usually stops in our dressing room so that we can concentrate on that which lies ahead. And I would like to think that our performance on the field is as good as that given by any other team of officials in the world, but that we also tend to take great enjoyment from such occasions.

Yet, despite the immense pleasure I get from refereeing, I couldn't possibly 'live' rugby every day of the week. I know of one young Welsh referee who comes home after a game and immediately analyses his performance that day on his laptop. He also studies other games in order to assess the referees involved. I could never do that, for I have to have an escape from the rugby field. When I worked at Maes yr Yrfa I had two hobbies: being an entertainer and a rugby referee. Now rugby is my job, and a very satisfying one at that, but I am so glad that entertaining, both as a comic and as an after-dinner speaker, provides me with such a pleasant distraction.

CHAPTER 4

Learning The Ropes

SINCE MAES YR YRFA was a comparatively small school, we often struggled to put a rugby team on the field, even when I was in the fifth form, or 'Year 11' as it is called today. However, that situation sometimes had its advantages, since it entailed that even I had a chance of making the team. In addition, one of my best friends, Craig Bonnell, was the captain, which meant that my hopes of getting selected were even higher. I really enjoyed playing each week, until that fateful game against Ysgol Gruffydd Jones, which in those days was a secondary school in St Clears. Before then we hadn't won a single game all season, yet we succeeded in scoring a late try to draw level at 12-12, leaving us with a conversion kick in front of the posts.

I was playing full-back on that occasion so I took the ball from Wayne Thomas, another good friend, who had just scored the try, and told Craig that I was going to take the conversion. I was, no doubt, anticipating the endless praise that would be heaped upon me if I was the one who ensured our first victory of the season. Unfortunately I didn't strike the ball cleanly at all and the kick sailed towards the corner flag! The Year 7 team had been playing on an adjacent pitch, and since their match had already finished they'd come to watch the exciting climax on our pitch, with the result that they witnessed my feeble conversion attempt. Some of them, for example Lee Scrace, Gari Thomas, Jonathan Clayton, Richard Babbs and Paul Davies (PD) are now close friends of mine and they still take pleasure in reminding me of that pathetic kick! Gari became a very good player and represented Swansea at full-back before injuries forced him to retire from the game. I would have loved to have had his talent but, then again, I wouldn't be where I am today if I had been any good as a player.

There were a few repercussions to that little disaster at St Clears. Craig didn't speak to me for a fortnight afterwards. Secondly, the late John Beynon, the games master, asked me if I would like to consider being a referee instead of trying to play the game. I had the greatest respect for John and in due course I became good friends with him and his family. He was one of the best – a teacher for whom nearly every child in school had the greatest respect. He put in a huge amount of work and spent a great deal of time on behalf of the pupils, both during and outside school hours. This was particularly true of rugby activities, and I began to referee most of the rugby matches that John arranged. There is no doubt that this helped me gain valuable experience as I climbed the refereeing ladder. When he was forced to retire due to ill-health, both Maes yr Yrfa and schools rugby in Wales suffered a great loss.

The more I thought about John's suggestion, the more it appealed to me. So when James Rees, another member of staff, showed me a poster which stated that the WRU were looking for referees and that a two-day course to train prospective referees was to be held in Cardiff, I was very keen to get involved. So, John Beynon and James Rees were instrumental in my deciding to become a referee. John had a prominent part to play in developing the rugby careers of other pupils as well, for example Dwayne Peel, Gareth Williams (a former captain of the Wales seven-a-side team) and more recently the likes of Lee Williams, a Pontyberem boy who is making a name for himself with the Scarlets and who I think deserves to get greater opportunity to show how good he really is.

However, my hopes of becoming a referee suffered a setback in the first instance. I was informed that those wishing to attend the course in Cardiff had to be 18 years old and that only by succeeding on that course could anyone hope to progress through the ranks of WRU referees. Yet I took a little comfort from the fact that I would be allowed to referee West Wales League games involving Llanelli and District clubs, which included many second teams of local union senior clubs. Alan Rees, whose parents Tal and Rita kept the post office in Mynyddcerrig, was an established referee and had been in charge of games involving some of the bigger clubs, such as Swansea and Llanelli. Alan took me to my first ever meeting, held at Furnace Rugby Club, of the Llanelli and District Rugby Union Referees Society, of which I have been chairman for many years.

We meet once a month as a society of referees and we all have an opportunity to discuss our experiences in recent games in which we have officiated. We now get together at Carmarthen Quins RFC. During the season we have specific sessions which I, as a professional referee, will take, involving the training of other referees. (I shall also be doing this with the other eight referees' societies within Wales). Our monthly meetings also give us a chance to get the opinion of other referees on certain decisions and to have a discussion on mistakes which some might have made during recent matches. For we all make mistakes from time to time, myself included. What's important is that we learn from those mistakes. I remember being told by the great Derek Bevan, a good friend and my refereeing coach, that there is nothing wrong with making a mistake; it's when you make the same mistake again that you have a problem.

In that first meeting of the society I was given a copy of the laws of the game and was able to meet and have a chat with Alun West concerning the way in which the society operated. He is a lovely, kind old gentleman who at that time was responsible for arranging the Llanelli and District League matches. He is now the President of the Llanelli District Union and he and the likes of Onfil Pickard and Ellis Davies were a great help to many referees like me over the years.

In the first instance, Alun asked me to take charge of a

game between Carmarthenshire and Pembrokeshire schools at Fivefields, which is where Carmarthen Athletic used to play but is now the site of a Tesco superstore. It is sad to think that a superstore now stands on the field where I refereed my first ever rugby match outside Maes yr Yrfa school. A sign of the times, perhaps. On that occasion, the game went better than I'd expected. So much so that one of the spectators, who had some official connection with schools rugby in the area, came up to me after the game and said, 'Well done! I thought you refereed the game very well. I believe you could go far as a referee.' At the time I was able to draw great encouragement from that compliment.

But I experienced a few problems at the beginning. When I asked Alun West if I could be given an opportunity to referee a few games, my only proviso was that I be allocated matches fairly close to home so that I could get to the venues in question without undue difficulty. For my father, who is not the best of drivers, did not like to drive long distances and was certainly not capable of dealing with hazards such as roundabouts. Since I was too young to drive, the only other option would be to get public transport or perhaps have my uncle Ken take me, which he subsequently did on many, many occasions. But the message obviously hadn't registered with Alun, since the first league game I was given was to be played in Tregaron, where the home team were entertaining Nantgaredig.

How was I to get to Tregaron, about an hour's drive from Mynyddcerrig? Alun West suggested that I ask Nantgaredig if I could have a lift on their team coach. So I rang the secretary to inform him of my dilemma and the club were very helpful and happy enough for me to travel with the team. However, when we arrived at Tregaron I decided to climb out through the fire exit window of the bus so that home team would not see me arriving on the visitors' coach. Tregaron lost 6-9 and there were no complaints from either team. After the game, I went back to the clubhouse for a pint and something to eat and all was well. That is, until it was time for the Nangaredig team to leave and their chairman shouted, 'Nigel, are you ready? The bus is leaving in two minutes!' I bolted out of the club and hurried onto the team coach. As it left the car park, I remember seeing a row of Tregaron players standing in the window, gesticulating angrily in my direction! So I eventually decided to get off the bus and get a lift back in a car with one of the players from Nantgaredig – but I don't think that fooled any of the Tregaron players!

A similar situation arose later on in that season. My parents had gone out for the day to visit family and my uncle Ken was on holiday in north Wales, with the result that I was stuck for a lift to the match. So I travelled on the Cefneithin team coach to Johnstown in Carmarthen, where they were playing against Division B of the South Wales Police. This time I was seen arriving with the visitors, and the police team made much of that fact during the game. Things didn't go their way that afternoon and during the second half, after I had penalised them yet again, their captain led his team from the field, saying that they didn't want to carry on playing. I had been brought up to believe that it was important to treat the police with respect, but as far as I was concerned, that respect was not due to them following a game which left me feeling quite downhearted concerning my future as a rugby referee. After all, I was just a sixteen-year-old schoolboy and to be treated in that way by grown up, supposedly responsible men was very upsetting at the time. Yet it was a pleasure being able to order fifteen burly policemen about the field for an hour or so; that brought a smile to my face for some time afterwards.

The person in charge of the police team that day was Brian Phillips, who was a policeman himself. He looked after me following the game and made a point of telling me not to worry about what had happened on the field, for which I was very grateful. These days he has the task of arranging referees for the Llanelli and District matches and he does a great job.

In fact he has been doing such a good job that he has been promoted to a new position: the Scarlets Region Referee Co-ordinator.

On the Monday following the match, Onfil Pickard, a very quiet and kind gentleman who had himself been a referee for many years (as well as a respected cricket umpire), made a point of coming to see me in school. At the time he was responsible for assessing the district referees and he wished to apologise for the conduct of the police team. He promised that such behaviour would not be tolerated in the future.

Uncle Ken once drove me to a match in Aberaeron and accidentally locked his keys in the car. As we were trying to resolve the problem, a young lad sauntered across the car park and told us he would get us into the car, no bother, as long as we looked away when he did so. He took something out of his pocket and proceeded to unlock Ken's car. We were very grateful, of course, but were a little worried about the safety of other vehicles in Aberaeron at the time!

If it hadn't been for Uncle Ken, I wouldn't have been able to get to all of the games which I refereed during that first season, so I owed him a great debt of gratitude. I still miss him greatly following his death at the beginning of 2008. I was so glad in recent years to have had the opportunity to repay him for his kindness to some degree, for I used to take him with me, along with my father and Roy Owen, a family friend from Mynyddcerrig, when I was officiating in some important matches. Usually the clubs in question would allow my passengers to come in with me to the stadiums concerned. There were exceptions, for example Llanharan RFC, who insisted that they paid the admission charge in full. Derek Bevan, who was with us in the car that day, remarked that he had never before witnessed that kind of attitude in all his years of refereeing. Was this, I wondered, one of the down sides of the game turning professional? I should add that the hosts lost the game that day, but it was a completely fair result!

I had important lessons to learn as a referee in those early days. I remember being in charge of a cup semi-final match between two great rivals: Carmarthen Quins Youth, who had Stephen Jones playing at outside half, and Carmarthen Athletic Youth. I had cause to warn one of the Quins players for a fairly serious offence but I forgot to note the number on his jersey. Soon afterwards I believed he was guilty of the same offence again so I called him over and was going to send him off. However, I then made the mistake of turning my back on him and walking in-field away from the touchline and the spectators. When I turned around to face him again there were two identical players standing before me, both of whom were smiling broadly. The 'offender' was one of the Morgan twins and I hadn't noticed up until then that it was impossible to tell one from the other. They knew full well that I was in no position to send either of them off, since I wasn't sure which twin had been given a warning and which had committed the second offence! So I learned that when telling an offender to approach me, I should walk backwards away from him. I see the twins in town from time to time and they often remind me of that incident. On the other hand, it might be that I encounter the same twin every time!

In fact, raking up past grievances seems to be a popular pastime when I go to Carmarthen. The following year I refereed a local cup final between the same two teams, with Stephen Jones once again playing outside half for the Quins. Towards the end of the game the Athletic centre, Darren Simpson, was tackled heavily and, according to some, the ball was knocked from his grasp in the direction of his own line. It was gathered by a member of his own team who crossed for a try, which appeared to seal the victory for Athletic. But I had a different take on the incident. In my opinion Darren had knocked the ball forward, with the result that I disallowed the try. To this day Darren swears that I robbed his team of a win and he continually claims to have a tape which confirms the fact. Each time I meet him in town I have to buy him a compensatory pint, but he has yet to produce the crucial video evidence!

In my early days as a referee many a crafty veteran, whose best days on the rugby field had long gone, would turn out for the second teams of some of the local clubs. They would usually take great pleasure in giving the bloke with the whistle a really hard time. They would try to influence the way in which I was running the game and continually question my decisions, all of which turned the pleasure of being a referee into a chore. Therefore, before long, acting in response to advice which I had been given by Alun West and Onville Pickard, I learned to be quite strict with these hasslers and to punish them as soon as they started their intimidating tactics. From then on I was allowed to get on with what I enjoyed doing most. I make a point even today of drawing upon that particular piece of advice, regardless of how well-known the culprit might be.

I once refereed a game between Glynneath and Cydweli. Both teams had their share of crafty veterans but one member of the Glynneath back row had been giving me a hard time from the start, probably because I appeared to be a fairly raw 22-year-old. The home side was leading by two points and this chap kept on asking, 'How much time, Ref?' or 'Time, Ref?' while pointing to his wrist. In that particular instance, penalising him would have been rather harsh, especially since the score was so close and there were only five minutes left. So I decided that if he asked again, I was going to shut him up. Just before the next scrum went down he again pointed to his wrist and shouted, 'Time, Ref? Ref, man, time?' I replied, in rather a matter-of-fact tone, 'Five to four, mate!' Both teams burst out laughing, but not the wing forward. 'Very funny!' was his only response. One of his colleagues added, 'What do you expect, he's a comedian on *Noson Lawen!*' I still use that line, even in high-profile matches, and it still gets a laugh!

When I was eighteen years old, I refereed a game at Maes yr Yrfa when a lad called Richard Lewis was playing in the school team. His brother, known as 'Stato' to us local lads, was in the same school class as me and was a good friend. His father, Humphrey, used to play flanker for Llanelli and was on the touchline, watching his son play. As was his custom he gave the referee quite a bit of stick, but I have to confess that after the game he gave me a piece of advice that I have valued ever since. There was some fighting during the game so I lectured the person I thought was responsible. This is what Humphrey told me: 'When I played, some offences were committed which weren't all that serious and generally didn't need to be penalised. For example, if an opponent was all over me in the line-out with his elbows, I would give him a little dig in the side as a warning not to do it again, an action which would sometimes be witnessed by the referee. But I had much more respect for a referee who would come up beside me, whilst we were perhaps running to the next breakdown or just as the next line-out was forming, and quietly tell me that he had seen what I had done and that he would therefore be keeping an eye on me for the rest of the game, than for a referee who liked giving public lectures on the field.' I have tried to bear his comments in mind ever since because what he said made a lot of sense.

Interestingly enough, I also received some sound advice from Humphrey's brother, Eldon, who was the secretary of Pontyberem Rugby Club for 26 years. I was seventeen at the time and was refereeing a game between Pontyberem Seconds and Amman United Seconds. When I was having a thirst-quenching drink in the clubhouse after the game, Eldon came over for a chat, during which he advised me never to referee with the whistle too near to my lips. He referred to a well-respected ex-international referee from Wales called Gwynne Walters, who usually wore a blazer on the field. He, apparently, always kept his whistle in his blazer pocket so that when he was inclined to blow, the two-second delay gave him time to reflect whether the incident in question required him to intervene at all. As a result, that short interval would often lead to his deciding to let play continue, whereupon the whistle was returned to his pocket. That illustration has served me well over the years, in that I always hold the whistle fairly low so I won't be tempted to blow up prematurely for something which would be better ignored. Unfortunately Eldon passed away in 2007. In appreciation of all his efforts on behalf of Pontyberem Rugby Club and as a token of my gratitude for his valued advice at all times, I wore a black arm band when I took charge of the EDF match between Bath and Cardiff Blues which was televised live, shortly after his death.

I have always thought it important for referees to listen to former players. I learned a lot about what went on in the front row by talking to ex-props or hookers, particularly when I was starting out. They were the ones who could advise me as to what I should be looking for when trying to decide who was responsible for collapsing a scrum. Therefore, I have always made a point of going to the clubhouse for a pint after a game so that I get a chance to chat with some former players who used to 'toil on the coal face' as it were. Even at the highest level, referees are able to profit from the advice of ex-players. A few years ago, Jon Humphries, the former Wales hooker and a respected coach, came to talk to the referees on the WRU panel on the art of scrummaging at our conference in Cardiff. Although we valued his contribution, we realised that he couldn't reveal everything, for he was aware that some of his audience, sometime in the future, would probably have to referee a team which was being coached by him. I am also grateful to Robin McBryde with whom I recently had a one-on-one session, so that I might learn more about some of the intricacies of front-row play.

One ex-member of the front-row fraternity who has given me sound and valuable advice on the complexities of that particular aspect of the game is Paul Lloyd, who played hooker and prop for Trimsaran and Pontyberem. He watches most of the games I referee on television and sometimes telephones me afterwards to discuss any problems he might have noticed or perhaps offer a few suggestions by sending me a text message. I am very grateful to those who have shown a willingness to assist in that way. After all, no one is ever too old to learn, and that is particularly true of rugby referees. I've also been giving some advice to young referees lately, guys like Craig Evans, a polite and pleasant lad from Glynneath, who I'm sure has a bright future ahead of him. I've been lucky to have great help and advice from peers over the years, so it gives me pleasure to give a little bit back and help referees who I hope will continue the great tradition of Welsh referees.

When I started refereeing I only had one jersey, a yellow one, which was a replica of Australia's rugby shirt. I still have it at home. Then after a few years I bought a green shirt and, since I was a member of the Llanelli and District Referees Society, I was entitled to wear the official badge of the Society of Welsh Rugby Union Referees, which bore the letters WSRUR. I was very proud of that shirt and wore it on every possible occasion, but in case one of the teams were wearing green jerseys, I always carried the yellow one with me.

One day I arrived to take charge of a game between Betws Seconds and Nantgaredig Seconds, to find that one of the teams would be playing in green and the other in yellow – a problem which called for a quick solution. The Betws boys, fortunately, came to the rescue. On the clubhouse wall was a glass case housing the jersey which a Betws player, the prop Arwyn Thomas, had worn when representing Wales at under-19 level. They kindly removed the international shirt from the case so that I could wear it to referee the game. That, however, didn't excuse me from getting some stick from the home contingent. For example, when I penalised Betws for collapsing the scrum, someone in the crowd shouted, 'You may be wearing a prop's jersey, but you know f*** all about reffin' them.' Ever since that day I have made a point of checking in advance the colours of both teams in any game that I am due to referee.

Now I have an extensive choice of rugby jerseys, mainly because different competitions and leagues require the referee to wear specific shirts which usually give prominence to the logos of various sponsors. The IRB referees kit at the moment is sponsored by Canterbury, and each season they send me three differently coloured jerseys, three pairs of shorts, three pairs of socks and a tracksuit. I am given a set of the same items for the Six Nations tournament, but this time with the RBS logo prominently displayed on them. For the Heineken Cup we used to have the Webb Ellis company sponsor us, but now Adidas have taken their place. They provide me with six jerseys, socks, shorts, a tracksuit, wetsuit undergarments and a T-shirt. Three of those shirts bear the logo 'Heineken Cup' and the others just 'H Cup', because advertising alcohol or tobacco is not permitted in France. The referees' kit for the Magners League is provided by Rhino, and features the name of the league's other sponsor, Specsavers. Their kit is made up of two jerseys, two pairs of shorts and socks, a tracksuit, wet-weather gear and a T-shirt. The WRU is sponsored by Underarmour and for union matches I receive jerseys, shorts and stockings each season, with the name of the other sponsor, SWALEC, prominently displayed on them. The Gilbert company provide me with kit for the EDF games and, for premiership games in Wales, I get a jersey sponsored by Principality. In addition, last season, Kooga supplied me with rugby boots, as well as other items of kit. In that connection I'm very grateful to Matt Fielding for the company's support. This year, though, I have been sponsored by Underarmour to wear their boots and kit whenever I'm refereeing, training or undertaking duties on behalf of the company or the WRU, and I'm very grateful to them for their support and to Craig Maxwell, one of their representatives, for his help.

As you can imagine, all that kit calls for a wardrobe of some considerable size. But I usually pass the previous season's issues on to the young lads who referee in the Llanelli District and to friends in the Pontyberem club. On some training nights you'd think that there was a team of referees on the field!

These days I quite often get requests for an autographed shirt in aid of a particular charity or good cause, or on the occasion of a notable event in the rugby world. For example, I presented the shirt I wore when refereeing England against the All Blacks to Machynlleth Rugby Club on the opening of their new clubhouse. The jersey I wore to referee the 2008 Heineken Cup final between Munster and Toulouse went to Aberystwyth Rugby Club, to be sold at an auction to raise money for the family of one of their players who'd lost his life in a road accident. It was great to hear that that particular shirt was sold for £700. Apparently it is displayed these days in one of the town's public houses. I was glad to hear also that a jersey I had given for auction in 2007, at a dinner for Welsh referees, had raised £300 for the Bryan 'Yogi' Davies Fund. Bryan received a serious injury a few years ago when playing for Bala Rugby Club.

When I sign a jersey I usually write on it the date of the match for which it was used, so that the person acquiring it knows that it is the genuine article and that there is only one in existence. It's only fair that you 'get what you pay for'. On one occasion I was asked by Alan Thomas, the secretary of Maesteg Quins RFC (who also works for the WRU), if I would be so kind as to donate a jersey to his club so that it could be put on display there. I told him that it would be a pleasure, and that the jersey in question would be the one I wore for my first Six Nations match: England v Italy at Twickenham. So I signed it: 'Eng. v Italy, 6 Nations 2007, Pob Hwyl, Nigel Owens.' (I always sign *pob hwyl*, which is 'best wishes' in Welsh, no matter for whom I'm signing or what country I happen to be in). However, when I gave the jersey to Alan, he thanked me for it and then looked at it with a rather puzzled expression. He asked, 'Are you sure that this is the jersey you wore for this match?' 'Yes,' I replied, 'of course it is! Why, what's wrong with it?' 'Well,' he said, 'this jersey is white – don't England play in white?' I had signed the wrong jersey, so I had to go home and get him the orange one that I had actually worn at Twickenham. The white one is still in the house and is often the subject of a few laughs when I tell friends the tale of my mistake. I am still not sure what to do with it, but maybe after this disclosure it will fetch a little more at a charity auction that it would otherwise have done!

What I don't like doing is asking for a jersey, an autographed programme or a ball from players. This can be quite embarrassing for a referee, but I have made one or two exceptions in the past. Last season Zoe, the Irish wife of my friend Gary Thomas who is a keen Munster supporter, asked me if I could get the team captain, Paul O'Connell, to autograph the match programme when I was refereeing them. She wanted to give it to her little boy, Brion. So after their game against the Gwent Dragons I had a word with Paul, who is a very pleasant person despite the impression he might give on the field. Not only did he willingly autograph the programme, he got all of the Munster team to sign it as well.

On another occasion last year I got a message on Facebook from a lady called Donna Davies. She mentioned that her friend's 11-year-old grandson, Connor Brown, from Cwmbrân, had been badly affected by his father's suicide. It seemed that Connor was a keen Dragons supporter and Donna wondered whether I might be able to get the team to sign a card for him, with a suitable message such as 'Thinking of you' or 'Best wishes'. I told her that the next time I was refereeing at Rodney Parade, I would arrange to take Connor with me or, failing that, I would take him there myself to see a match and meet the players afterwards. And that's what happened.

The Dragons were playing the Scarlets in a Welsh derby at Newport, so on the night of the game I met Connor, his mother and Donna in Sainsbury's car park, then off we went to Rodney Parade. I'd been in touch with Gethin Jenkins and Paul Turner from the Dragons to ask if it was OK with them, and to their credit they were very happy to co-operate. They reserved seats for Connor and myself in the stand, arranged for us to go to the home changing room after the match to meet the players, then go upstairs to have food with them. They all signed Connor's autograph book and Tom Willis, the Dragons captain, gave him his training jersey. I let him have a tracksuit top that I sometimes wore when refereeing. He was delighted, and when I took him back to the car park I got a huge hug from both his mother and Donna which, I have to admit, made me feel rather tearful. This left Connor looking rather perplexed, for here was this soppy bloke whom he had often seen fearlessly ordering huge, aggressive players about the rugby field, now with a tear in his eyes and in the arms of two women!

Donna telephoned the following day to thank me and said that Connor's mother had telephoned her the following day to thank me too and to say that they'd already noticed a big change in Connor. He was much happier and he'd refused to take off the jersey which he'd been given by Tom Willis, even to go to bed. A few days later I received a card from Donna on which she'd written: 'Thank you very much for all that you've done in arranging the evening for Connor Brown. You are truly a wonderful person with a generosity of spirit that has no boundaries. With deepest gratitude to you.' Receiving such a message meant a lot to me and gives me far greater satisfaction than being lauded for refereeing a game of rugby well.

Although I try to be meticulous when packing my kit before a match, it's quite easy to overlook something. When I reached the changing room in Marseilles, where I was to run the line in the 2007 World Cup semi-final between Australia and England, I found that I had left my boots in the hotel in Paris. Luckily Marius Jonker from South Africa, the video referee that day, kindly offered to lend me his boots. However he wore size 12 and my size was 9, so I took to the field wearing three pairs of socks and having stuffed reams of paper inside the boots. To make matters worse, it was an extremely hot day so Marius's boots didn't smell all that sweetly when he got them back.

I learned early in my career what I should – or rather shouldn't – do *after* a game. When I was 17, I took charge of a game in Laugharne which the home team lost. As is the custom after the final whistle they stood on the touchline, in two rows, to applaud the winners off the field. I followed, walking off between the two lines of Laugharne players, who in turn left the field after me. That is when the home 'sponge man' came up quietly behind me and gave me a vicious blow in the back. I did nothing about it at the time, but with hindsight I should have reported the person in question so as to make sure it would not happen to another referee there in the future. Ever since, I have ensured that I am the last person to walk off the pitch after a game, or that I keep my distance from players and officials as I leave the field on my own! I didn't get much of a welcome in the Laugharne clubhouse that evening. Strangely enough I returned there five months later to referee a game which the home team won. I was very well received in the club on that occasion; indeed, I could have stayed there for the whole weekend if I had wanted!

There were two other young referees trying to gain experience in the Llanelli and District games at the same time as me, namely Wayne Davies from Felinfoel, who became a good friend, and Carwyn Phillips, who was manager of the Co-op in Llandeilo. Our aim was to get promoted to West Wales Rugby Union referees, so the Llanelli and District Referees Society had been assessing us regularly throughout the season. However, before we could be considered for promotion, we were required to complete the referees course held in Cardiff, to which I referred earlier. But the year I became old enough to attend (18), a celebrity soccer match had been arranged on the very evening of the course, between Maes yr Yrfa staff and the cast of *Pobol y Cwm*. I wasn't going to miss out on such a special occasion, so I decided to play in the match and to delay my attendance on the course until the following year.

After the course, by which time I was 20 years old, Gwyn Watts, the official referees assessor, was going to decide which of the three Llanelli and District junior referees would be promoted. He came to see me refereeing the final of the Llanelli and District Youth Cup competition between Llandovery and Carmarthen Quins. I must have done quite well on the night because I was the one who got promoted; yet apparently just two marks separated Wayne, Carwyn and myself. As it happened, they too were promoted within the next two years. I was now 21 years old and a referee with the West Wales Rugby Union, making me eligible to take charge of matches involving clubs which played in the union's lower divisions.

The system employed by the union to grade referees allows them to gradually progress through the ranks and, if they are good enough, to reach the top. I was moving up from the Llanelli District to become a Grade 4 Probation referee under the union's scrutiny. The next step would be to move steadily up through the grades and divisions so that, if I was promoted every season, I would go from 4 Probation to 4, 3, 2b, 2a, 1 and from there, finally, onto the panel of top referees. Now the system has changed slightly but it is still pretty much the same, apart from the names of the grades. If you are a premiership referee now, you will referee games in the Welsh Premiership Division and maybe the odd Magners League game. Then, if you progress further, you get on the panel of referees who take charge of representative matches, Heineken Cup games and international fixtures, which would be the pinnacle for any Welsh referee. Little did I know or think, whilst slowly but gradually progressing through the grades, that this would happen to me in a few years' time.

CHAPTER 5

Making A Mark

WHEN I STARTED OUT, every referee was assessed at least three or four times a year by a former referee appointed by the union, or by the district in the case of those who hadn't yet got on to the lowest rung of union referees. The system has changed a little now, with district referees coming under the control of the WRU and its Community Referees Manager, David Davies, a former international referee who is working hard to promote new and young referees in particular. Each referee is marked on various aspects of his performance throughout the season and will be seen by a few different assessors during the course of the year. The assessors then will meet as a group under the watchful eye of Robert Yeman, the WRU Match Officials Manager, and make a decision as to whether a particular referee is good enough to be promoted to a higher level.

While progressing through the ranks I learned many important lessons, some of which, on reflection, were quite funny. I remember refereeing a local cup match between Resolven and Seven Sisters just before Christmas. I'd heard that Clive Norling, who was at that time in charge of referees on behalf of the WRU, was going to be there, so it was important that I put in a decent performance. I had quite a good game but at one point I had cause to send Darren Davies, the Resolven flanker, to the sin bin for ten minutes. Now, the sin bin had been a problem for the union for some time. According to the rules, any player who got three yellow cards in a season would be suspended for a period. However, the system was ineffective because referees often failed to notify the union of the names of the players they'd sent to the sin bin during recent games. As a result, the authorities were unable to keep track of the players who got three yellow cards. So there was a campaign in force to get referees to do their duty and submit the names of players who were sin binned in any game. It was my practice never to ask for names of offending players during the course of a game, since the whole process of getting that information and writing it down, in my opinion, was an unwelcome interruption to the run of play. In addition, asking a player for his name could run the risk of my getting an answer similar to the one given to me by a Mountain Ash player after I'd shown him a yellow card, namely 'Mickey F***ing Mouse'!

So normally I would just note the number on the player's jersey and, when I got back to the changing room after the game, link it to the corresponding name on the official team sheet which every team, in accordance with union rules, is obliged to display before the teams take the field. In this particular instance, I got back to the changing room to find that no team sheet was displayed there. It appeared that since the game in question was a local cup match, the union rule did not apply. What, therefore, was I going to do now, particularly in the light of the fact that Clive Norling had witnessed the player in question being sent to the sin bin and that I wasn't in a position to forward his name? To top it all, Clive came into the changing room after the game to tell me that I'd done well. So I had to find a rapid answer to my problem.

After I got home I telephoned the Resolven club and asked to speak to the secretary. There was no point in my trying to get him to tell me the name of the player who'd been shown the yellow card, for, in true secretarial tradition, he would have refused! So I decided to draw upon the limited talent that I have as an impersonator for the conversation that was to follow, which went something like this:

'Hello, it's Mark Orders here from the *South Wales Evening Post.*'

'Hiya, Mark, how are you?' replied the secretary.

'Fine thanks. Can you confirm the score of today's game for me?'

'We won 15-9,' he said, and proceeded to list the scorers.

'I believe there was a yellow card?'

'Yes, Darren Davies got sin binned.'

'Right. Thanks very much. Oh, by the way, what was the ref like?'

'F***ing useless,' he replied.

And this was after Resolven had won! That was the first and last time that I asked a club official for an opinion on my performance.

I can note one fact about yellow cards which could be used for a good quiz question: I was the first rugby referee in Wales to issue a yellow card – in a game between Trebanos and Trimsaran. In those days the sin bin didn't exist and the yellow card served as a warning. Since one of the Trebanos lads was getting married on the Saturday, the club had asked if the match could take place the previous Friday evening. During the game I had cause to show the yellow card to Andrew Thomas, one of the Trimsaran players, the day before any other referee had a chance to take it out of his pocket.

Over the years, I succeeded in moving up steadily from division to division. At the end of one season I managed to leapfrog a division, but that was due to a stroke of luck. I was refereeing at the time in Division 3 and I was being assessed on a regular basis by the former referee, Keith 'Mogo' Jones. He told me towards the end of the season that he was going to send one of the union assessors to see me refereeing Penygraig against Senghenydd and, on the basis of my performance on that day, a decision would be made as to whether I was good enough to move up to Division 2. At that time Clive Norling, who'd had an outstanding career as a referee, had just resumed duties as an assessor with special responsibilities for nurturing eight or nine young referees who, in his opinion, had the ability to reach the top in due course. As it happened, I wasn't one of them. Before long, this exclusive little group were being referred to as 'Norling's Angels' – some of whom eventually became high fliers; for example, Nigel H Williams, Nigel Whitehouse, Paul Adams and Huw Watkins.

During the morning of the game, Clive telephoned me to confirm where exactly it was being played and at what time. Indeed, I could see him sitting in the stand when I ran onto the field and I had taken it for granted that Keith Jones had asked him to come and run the rule over me. However, I had quite a shock after the game when another assessor, Steve Jeffries, walked into the changing rooms and announced that he was the independent assessor whom Keith had asked to attend and that he wished to discuss my performance with me. He told me that he hadn't been all that impressed with the way I had refereed and that he wished to draw attention to a few of my shortcomings. For example, there were a few offside offences in midfield which I had failed to penalise. His advice to the union, as a result, would be that I remained as a Division 3 referee for at least another season. At that point the changing room door opened and Clive Norling came in. Both he and Steve Jeffries were a little taken aback to find that the two of them had come to the same game.

'How did you think it went?' Clive asked me. I thought to myself, I'll be clever here now and mention the faults Steve Jeffries had pointed out, so I cautiously answered, 'Not bad, but I might have missed a few offsides in midfield. I think I need to work on that aspect of my game a bit more.' Whereupon he consulted his notes and said, 'Not at all. I've got you down for very good scanning of midfield. No, it went very well.' I saw Steve Jeffries' jaw drop but he didn't say a word. On the basis of Clive's report, I was promoted from Division 3 directly to Division 1. Were it not for the fact that he had happened to drop in on that particular match, I might still be refereeing in Division 3 today. After that game I, too, became one of Norling's Angels.

Yet the referees assessment and training system operated by the WRU is a source of considerable admiration and it's good to see that so many former successful referees, such as Derek Bevan, Clayton Thomas, Malcolm Thomas, Les Peard, Jim Bailey, Ken Rowlands, Alun Richards, Tony Lynch, Vernon Brown and, previously, Gwyn Watts are making an important contribution to its success. They were all a great help to me over the years. I was always particularly appreciative of Gwyn's style of assessment. He would go over various aspects of the game and would give me an opportunity to justify any of my decisions with which he might have disagreed, whilst always being prepared to change his opinion in the light of my explanation. There were other assessors, however, who would never be prepared to consider an alternative argument, insisting that their interpretation was the only possible explanation. Gwyn passed away in August 2008 and he will be greatly missed, not only in Welsh refereeing circles but throughout the rugby world. He was an official assessor in three World Cup competitions, and when I was chosen as a referee for the 2007 World Cup the first congratulatory letter that I received was from Gwyn Watts.

Every referee receives a written copy of his assessor's report a few days after each game. I have only once had cause to make an official complaint about an assessment. I was refereeing a Heineken Cup match between Saracens and Biarritz when I saw one of the French team's forwards taking a dramatic dive following a fairly innocuous push by one of his opponents. I called out to him, 'Come on, get up! You're in London now, not in Hollywood!' The assessor that day, Tony Trigg, had been appointed by the English Rugby Union. In his report he stated that he had deducted two marks from my overall score for the joke about Hollywood. He added that my comment had been inappropriate and, in any event, the reference to Hollywood would not have been understood by someone from France. In addition, he deducted another point due to my inability to communicate with the Biarritz players in French. I complained to the WRU Referees Manager, Robert Yeman, and raised the question whether a referee visiting Llanelli would be penalised for not being able to speak to any Scarlets player, whose first language was Welsh, in his native tongue. By the same token I asked whether referees were expected to be able to speak Russian in Russia, Afrikaans in South Africa or Italian in Italy. Robert brought these matters to the attention of Colin High, a fair and honest man, and his counterpart in the English Rugby Union, and as a result the marks which Tony Trigg had deducted from my score were restored.

These days language is not a problem on the rugby field. Most foreign players are familiar with the English terms that apply to the most important aspects of the game, but if a referee has cause to speak to an individual who does not understand much English, there is usually someone in his team who is able to translate for him. It's customary for a referee, when a foreign side is playing, to enquire before the game whether any member of that particular team is able to understand and speak English. Having said that, a tactic employed by some foreign sides is to claim that not one of their team understands what the referee is trying to say. I became aware of that early in my career when I was running the line in a Heineken Cup match between London Irish and Agen. The referee was Derek Bevan, and when he went into the French team's dressing room to ask how many were able to speak English, one of them replied, 'Only me, and just a *leetl* bit.' As we walked on to the pitch, Derek said to me, 'You watch, by the end of the game they'll all be able to speak English.' And he was right. After the final whistle a queue of Agen players approached us, making such comments as 'Thanks very much for an excellent game!' and 'Ref, thanks, we enjoyed that very much!'

Speaking Welsh on the field has been an issue at times. I

have been given to understand that some people are unhappy with the fact that during a game I might speak Welsh to, for example, Stephen Jones, Dwayne Peel, Shane Williams, Mefin Davies, Nicky and Jamie Robinson, Deiniol Jones, Kevin Morgan, Mike Phillips, Dafydd Jones, John Davies and Jamie Roberts. I do this not because I'm trying to make a point by speaking to players in Welsh but rather because it's completely natural for me to do so. But if I have reason to tell them something which other players need to understand I will then speak to them in English. I am proud of the Welsh language and I will speak it at every opportunity – in Wales or anywhere else in the world. One of my pet hates is to hear people who are fluent Welsh speakers talking in English to each other.

On the other hand, it's just as well sometimes that not everyone understands what's happening on the field. Once, during a game between the Blues and the Scarlets I awarded a penalty to the Cardiff team quite a distance from the posts. Nicky Robinson came up to me and said, in Welsh, 'I'm going for goal,' so I gave the appropriate sign to indicate his intention. Whereupon he laughed and immediately said, 'No, I'm only joking. I'm going for touch!' According to the laws, once a player has stated his intention with regard to the taking of a penalty he is not allowed to change his mind. So I could have told him that he was now obliged to kick for goal. However, since he was joking (a fact which I could appreciate upon realising that the mark was so far from the posts) and since, more importantly perhaps, none of the opposition had understood what he had said, I allowed him to kick for the corner.

I recently refereed a game in which Mefin Davies was playing hooker for Leicester. We were the only two Welsh speakers on the field, but throughout the game I communicated with him in Welsh, much to the confusion of the other players!

Of course, there are now quite a few Welsh players plying their trade outside Wales and I come across them quite often, especially during the Heineken Cup. On one occasion last year I was refereeing Munster v Sale at the new Thomond Park in Limerick, a great stadium which is always brimming with passion. There were two Welsh-speaking players in the Sale side that day, Eifion Roberts and Dwayne Peel. A few minutes into the second half Eifion, a burly prop forward, had just tackled Alan Quinlan, the Munster back rower, and was not moving off the ball or the ball carrier, so I penalised him. I told him in Welsh, 'Now, you know what you are doing, so move away from there more quickly, please.' He got up, shaking his head, as they usually do when you penalise them. Alan Quinlan, who was still on the ground, said with a smile on his face, 'I take it that meant 'move away'?' 'Yes,' I said, 'you got it!'

Another sensitive issue which referees constantly have to address is whether or not they should call players they know well by their Christian names. I tend to call only the captains by their Christian names, but if it's a match between two Welsh regions then I do so for all the players – assuming that I know who they all are, which is generally the case. However, during matches involving teams from outside Wales I usually refer to the players by the numbers on their jerseys rather than by their names, since it's more than likely that I wouldn't know most of their names and I certainly wouldn't be able to pronounce some of the foreign names properly. But the most important consideration in all of this is that the referee is consistent in the way in which he deals with both teams.

If I might return to the complaint made by the English assessor concerning my attempted joke, I am a great believer in using humour on the field whenever circumstances permit, for it can help to release tension. I once refereed a game in the World Sevens Championships in Hong Kong during which the Argentina scrum-half complained incessantly. I eventually got fed up of his antics and called him over. 'Listen,' I said, 'you've got two ears and one mouth. From now on use them in that proportion!' The other players were very amused and even the official assessor for the game expressed his appreciation of that particular comment. In another match, I frequently had cause to penalise a particular Penygraig player in their cup game against Pontypridd. As it happened he was cross-eyed, and at one stage, with the ball in his hands, he made a point of running directly into me, resulting in my being knocked to the ground. 'Why the hell don't you look where you're going?' was his comment, although fully aware that he had been the guilty party. I took great pleasure in replying, 'Why don't you go where you're looking?' – much to the amusement of the other players.

Perhaps I pushed my luck a little in a Blues v Dragons match. There hadn't been any problems at all in the scrums for sixty minutes, then both sides brought on front row substitutes: Hugh Gustafson for the Dragons and John Yapp for the Blues. The next three scrums collapsed on their side, so I called them both out and said, 'I can see now why you two are not starting the match!' The other players thought this was quite amusing but the two props didn't see the funny side. However, it had the desired effect since not a single scrum collapsed after that. Hugh, who is a Welsh speaker and played a few seasons for Pontyberem Youth, came to have a chat with me after the game and said. 'Nige, that was a bit harsh, people at home will now think I can't scrummage'. I said, 'Hugh bach, if you thought I was going to let them think I can't referee you've got another thing coming!'

In a youth match between Pontyberem and Cydweli, early during my career as a referee, there had been quite a bit of fighting. When another eruption occurred, with the brothers Matthew and Phil Rowe (who are good friends of mine) threatening to get involved, I warned them to keep away. I shouted, 'Walk this way or you're walking that way!' whilst pointing towards the changing rooms. For years afterwards, whenever I refereed at Pontyberem (which is my home club, of course) and there was a bit of a dust-up on the field, some of my friends who witnessed the original incident would shout out, 'Walk this way or you're walking that way!' It even happens when I am only a spectator there! I go to watch Pontyberem play at every opportunity, although that's a fairly rare occurrence these days, and I'm sure to get some stick while standing on the touchline. For example, another friend of mine, Peter Lewis (or 'Peter Pig' as he's called locally), always takes great delight in shouting loudly during quiet moments something like: 'Hey, Nigel, it's only the good refs that are on duty today, then!'

I've often had cause to smile at some of the comments directed at me from the crowd. Naturally enough, I was an easy target when I used to appear regularly on *Noson Lawen*, particularly if I happened to referee a game on the day following the programme. 'Hey, Owens,' shouted a spectator at Whitland one Saturday, 'you were supposed to be a comedian last night, not this afternoon!'

There are quite a few characters amongst the players, some of whom are able to relieve tension with a funny comment. Tom Shanklin has a very dry sense of humour which often gives rise to a smile. Alan Quinlan, the Munster player, is another who makes me laugh, usually by trying to act the innocent when I know full well that he realises exactly what he's about! I particularly remember a comment by Conor O'Shea, the former London Irish full-back, which tickled me. I'd penalised him for a high tackle, to which he responded by exclaiming, 'But Ref, he ran into my arm!' I could have replied, 'Yes, which was high, stiff, and waiting for him!' but I settled for giving just a penalty against him. In that instance his humorous reaction probably saved him from getting a yellow card. By now I've learnt that I should deal with the incident and not the intent of the player, and that my judgement should not be swayed by a funny comment! Unfortunately, one hears considerably fewer funny comments in the modern game compared to years ago. One reason for this is that many of today's big matches are televised, for which the referees wear a microphone, with the result that both the ref and the players have to be very careful with regard to what they say.

Nevertheless, despite the importance of humour on the field of play, a delicate balance must be struck between being funny and being serious. It is not the time to crack a joke when someone deserves a lecture for dirty play or when a prop, perhaps, has run twenty yards to cross the try line, only to knock on as he's trying to ground the ball. In addition, any humorous comment by the referee must come naturally. I'm fortunate in that it's not difficult for me to relax during a game now, and I find that the greater the pressure due to the importance of the game, the better I referee. I felt rather pleased two seasons ago, after the Heineken Cup quarter-final between Munster and Gloucester, when one of the senior officials of the referees' hierarchy congratulated me not only on the standard of my refereeing that afternoon but also on my general performance out in the middle.

In my opinion, if a referee is going to gain the respect of the players, he must himself show respect towards them. He should always be decisive and should never try to guess what may have happened. In addition he must be honest at all times and if he makes a mistake he should be man enough to admit it. A few seasons ago, in an important game between the Scarlets and the Ospreys, I sent Mike Phillips to the sin bin for what I thought at the time was a late and dangerous tackle. When I watched the video of the game later that week, as I am required to do as part of my work and self-assessment programme, I realised that I should have awarded a penalty for Mike's offence but not a yellow card. A few days later I was refereeing a game between the Ospreys and the Blues. Part of the officials' pre-match duties is to check the players' boots and clothing to make sure they all comply with International Rugby Board (IRB) requirements. We also talk to the front rows so that they are all aware of the scrum safety requirements.

Whilst I was in the changing rooms, Mike asked me if I had seen the yellow card incident again. No doubt to his surprise, I said, 'Yes, Mike, I have and I'm sorry about the yellow card, for I got it wrong. It should have been just a penalty.' Nevertheless I appreciate the need to be careful when deciding to apologise. For example, I would never go into the changing room of a team that had just lost a Heineken Cup semi-final to apologise for the fact that I hadn't seen the opposition knock the ball on when crossing the line for the try that won them the game in the last minute!

I remember showing a yellow card to Andrew Thomas (the same chap who got the first ever yellow card when playing for Trimsaran a few years earlier) in a cup match between Newport and Aberavon. By this time getting a yellow card meant spending ten minutes in the sin bin, and if a player received three such cards in a season he would be suspended for a period. On behalf of their player, Aberavon appealed against my decision and I was required to attend a subsequent hearing in Cardiff. When I arrived and went into the hearing, I was informed of the grounds on which the appeal was based. I was shown a replay of the incident and came to the conclusion myself that I might have been wrong. In fact I *was* wrong. Yet when I was asked during the hearing whether I considered that my reaction might have been too severe, I refuted that suggestion. However, it was obvious to the officials at the hearing that Andrew had been wrongly sin binned and he won his appeal. After the meeting, one of the officials told me to remember that there was no harm in admitting sometimes to being wrong. Ever since that evening, therefore, I have always tried to be honest with myself and with the players, so when I know I've made a mistake I apologise to them. I would like to think that, as a result, I've had far more respect from players and coaches alike.

On another occasion I had to go to Cardiff for an appeal hearing which was considering the case of Percy Montgomery.

He played for Newport then and I had sent him off in a league match in Swansea for pushing Peter Rees, one of the touch judges, to the ground after the home side had scored a try. I was shocked to hear, via our communication system, from Peter Rees and Richard Hughes, the other touch judge, what had happened. I called Montgomery towards me to tell him that he was being sent off, but as I was putting my hand in my pocket to get the red card out and to inform him of my decision, he just ran straight past me without waiting to hear his fate. Montgomery was hoping at the time that he would be recalled to the South Africa squad, with the possibility of World Cup selection a year later. The game in question was the last one between the two teams before they became regional clubs and I must say that it remains the most difficult game I've ever refereed as far as trying to maintain discipline was concerned. Two Newport players and one of the All Whites got red cards on the day.

The media worldwide had an interest in the story, since physically abusing a referee or a linesman was a serious offence for which a player, if found guilty, could receive a lengthy suspension or even a life suspension. The two touch judges and I were called to the appeal and fortunately, since the three of us were Welsh speakers, we were able to discuss things without most of the press being able to understand what we were saying.

The appeal had been arranged because Montgomery had claimed that Rees had sworn at him and that was why he had pushed him. I hadn't heard anything of the sort at the time, and to this day I still do not know what really happened, although I must admit I would not have had Peter down as an official who would swear at a player like that. On the other hand, if you were to ask me to draw up a list of ten players who were most likely to push an official over then Percy's name would not appear there either. The two crucial factors were that the Newport player had pushed Peter and that he had confessed to the offence. It was evident that the Appeals Committee were faced with the same dilemma as us officials.

Many letters were read out confirming that Percy Montgomery was a man who could be believed and trusted, one of which had been sent by Jonathan Kaplan, the international rugby referee from South Africa. After a lengthy discussion it was decided to suspend Montgomery for six months and that he should be fined a substantial amount. Only he and Peter Rees can explain what really happened behind the posts at St Helens that night. In my opinion the committee, having taken everything into account, came to the right decision.

There was a match at Sardis Road between Pontypridd and Cardiff during my early days as a referee, when I was perhaps a little too 'whistle happy'. It was one of my first games at that level and it was being televised live. It was a close, tense encounter with two former home club favourites, Neil Jenkins and Martyn Williams, now playing for the visitors. It was also pouring down with rain. At the end of the first half, Pontypridd were leading by seven points. I had penalised them three times and Cardiff about ten. As it was a derby match with me fairly inexperienced for a big occasion like this, I was keen to stamp my authority on the proceedings, but on reflection I failed to take the atrocious weather into consideration. I was too keen to penalise the teams for offences which I would probably overlook, or at least manage without giving a penalty these days. As I walked from the pitch at half time in the company of one of the touch judges, Huw Watkins, we came face to face with three of the Cardiff officials – Robert Norster, Dai Young and Gareth Edwards – as they left the stand. Neither Huw or I had ever met the great Gareth Edwards before, so Huw pushed in front of me to shake his hand. However, Gareth walked straight past him and up to me. Clearly exasperated, he exclaimed, 'For God's sake, give us *something* in the second half!'

Usually I am completely unfazed when the crowd gets

worked up over some of my decisions, but I've had reason to be concerned about my safety in some places, particularly in France and sometimes in South Africa. Often at French grounds you have to go through a caged walkway to get on to the field, which isn't a bad idea at all when you consider that some of the more passionate fans out there take great delight in throwing bottles and spitting at anyone who upsets them. I remember a post-match incident in Auch after the home team had lost, which to some extent was due to the fact that I had one of their players sent off. After getting changed, we found that there were about two hundred enraged Frenchmen waiting to vent their anger on us outside the dressing room. We were told that it would be unwise for us to go to the post-match function and were escorted by the local police out through the back door and into a waiting taxi, which took us straight back to the hotel. We were advised that it would be safer for us to stay in the hotel that night and not even venture to the local bars. Needless to say, we heeded their advice.

One of the most difficult places to referee in Wales was probably Stradey Park, although the home supporters there were angels in comparison with some foreign grounds. Yet Llanelli supporters are exceptionally partisan and they generally believe that since I only live down the road, all my decisions should favour the Scarlets. But Pontyberem is about nine miles from Llanelli and as a kid I was never a fan of the Scarlets or any other of the so-called 'big Welsh clubs'. Some fans from other regions and clubs say that I should not be allowed to referee the Llanelli club side or the Scarlets, but that would be tantamount to saying that someone living in Swansea could not referee Neath or the Ospreys or that someone from Pontypridd should not referee Cardiff or the Blues, as they are closer to each other than Pontyberem is to Llanelli. In every match I have ever refereed, no matter which teams were involved, I have always dealt fairly with both sides and treated both sets of players in the same way – which I shall continue to do. Now, don't get me wrong, if any of the Welsh regions were playing in a Heineken or EDF Cup match in which I was not involved, then naturally I would want them to win, but when I officiate in any capacity then I go into my neutral mode.

I remember refereeing Llanelli against Cardiff at Stradey Park, some two seasons before the regions were formed and about ten days before Graham Henry was to select the Wales team to play in a Six Nations match. Stephen Jones was playing outside half for the home team opposite Iestyn Harris, the visitors' fly-half. Since both were the subject of great public debate as to who would be picked to play for Wales at number ten in a fortnight's time, there was big-match atmosphere all around the nearly full ground. Just before half time I penalised one of the Stradey favourites, Garan Evans, right in front of the main stand. This led to a noisy chorus of 10,000 hoarse and irate Scarlets supporters. As Iestyn came up to take the kick he said to me, 'Don't let them get to you, Ref. Don't worry about it!' 'I'm not,' I said, 'they're booing you, not me.' In fact they were still booing when we came out for the second half.

There were many who said that I, as the number one referee in Wales, should have refereed the last match at Stradey, which was the Scarlets v Bristol in the Anglo-Welsh Cup. In fact I had a phone call from a reporter asking why that wasn't the case. My answer, quite simply, was that I couldn't dream of undertaking such a task. After all, what if the Scarlets lost with me in charge? I wouldn't be allowed to live it down! Mind you, in hindsight, it would have been an honour to be part of that great occasion at Stradey Park to say farewell to one of the most famous rugby grounds in the world.

To be honest, I'm not a big fan of these new multi-purpose stadiums, shared between rugby and football clubs. They may well be great state of the art stadiums but I think they loose a lot of the atmosphere and passion that one can only connect with at the traditional rugby stadiums. I would much prefer to referee in a rugby stadium packed with 12,000 rugby-mad spectators than a new 22,000 seater with less than 9,000 at the ground. If I as a referee feel this way then surely the players must also feel a difference.

Hearing someone say that I favoured a particular team really makes me annoyed. The matter raised its head again when Derwyn Jones, the former international second row, was part of S4C's Welsh language commentary team for the Leinster v Ospreys match which I was refereeing. At one point during the first half he claimed that I, unfortunately, tended to side with teams from Wales when refereeing games in which their opponents were from another country. Interestingly enough, during the BBC's English language broadcast of the same game, Robert Jones, the former international scrum-half, who was sharing coverage with Gareth Charles, one of the best rugby commentators on television in my view, made a point of noting that I never favoured either of the teams in any game in which I was the referee, regardless of who was involved. Of course, what coaches tend to forget is that an official independent assessor is present at every big game, and he has a duty to analyse in detail the referee's performance. It's an established fact that no assessor has ever noted that I favoured one particular team at the other's expense.

We all have our faults in this world but I can honestly say, hand on heart, that being dishonest or favouring one team more than the other has never entered my mind. My parents raised me to be agreeable, polite, courteous and honest – principles which have always been important to me – and I don't intend changing my ways now or in the future. Everyone has an opinion of me as a referee, and who knows how the rugby world will assess me in years to come? But I would like to think that all are agreed that Nigel Owens is always fair and honest when carrying out his duties on the rugby field.

I remember having quite an argument with one particular international coach, whom I shan't name because he's still active in that capacity. He stormed into my changing room after a game, complaining that I had failed to notice a forward pass by their opponents which led to a try that turned out to be a winning score. As it happened, I looked at a video of the game and it's possible that the pass concerned was forward, but it was difficult to say. The angle from which the movement is seen is crucial in coming to a decision on these matters, and my view is that if I am unsure about something then I should keep the whistle away from my mouth. So I asked the irate coach, 'How many penalties did your fly-half miss today?'

'Three,' he replied.

'How many conversions did he miss?'

'One.'

'How many times did he knock on?'

'Twice.'

'How many times did he die with the ball after ignoring an overlap outside him?'

'Twice,' he replied after a while.

'And you're blaming me for the fact that you lost!' I said rather heatedly. 'Now bugger off out of here and don't come back until you have reflected on things a little more professionally!'

And off he went with his tail between his legs.

In December 2001 I made the difficult decision to resign from my post as technician and leave Maes yr Yrfa, where I had spent eighteen happy years both as a pupil and as an employee, to become a full-time referee. If I hadn't made that choice, I could still be employed at the school today. During that period I spent a lot of time discussing my possible departure with people like Melody Gronw from the science department and Shân Ifans, who was head of geography. Sian Williams from the PE department and members of the administrative staff, such as Sharon, Bill and Robert Samms, also took part in the process. They tried to impress upon me the importance of taking the opportunity of becoming a professional referee, whilst stressing that declining to do so would be a decision that I would surely regret in due course. The financial advantages were not to be scoffed at. As a technician I earned about £14,000 per annum but as a referee my income would be much more.

My colleagues at Maes yr Yrfa certainly knew what they were talking about, for they had a shrewd understanding of the rugby world. For example, Shân Ifans was one of the Scarlets' most fervent supporters, and if I'd been refereeing at Stradey on the Saturday and the Scarlets had lost, she wouldn't be speaking to me in school on the following Monday. Sadly Shân passed away some five years ago, but her husband, Geoff, still kindly sends me text messages after some of the games I've refereed, and it's obvious that he's very glad of my success.

On my last day at Maes yr Yrfa I was presented with a number of gifts from staff and pupils alike. One was a piece of Welsh poetry written by Iwan Rhys, a pupil in Year 13 who had won many Eisteddfod prizes. It was a lovely poem and it takes pride of place at home today. But one of the most cherished gifts is a photo album from the staff which Shân was responsible for organising, as she always did when someone retired from the school. It contained photographs of all the staff, with a written comment from everyone. I still look back with great pride on the kind words that they all wrote.

In addition to getting paid for every game that I refereed, I had been offered a central contract by the WRU which meant that I would be receiving even more money. I was offered a two-year contract initially, after I'd been interviewed by some senior union representatives including the likes of Terry Cobner, Dennis Gethin, Glanmor Griffiths, Terry Vaux and Clive Norling, who was in charge of referees at the time. The fact that I was now a professional did not, of course, make me a better referee, and I could very well have carried on refereeing in addition to working as a school technician. Some referees at the highest level, such as Alain Rolland and Alan

Lewis, are still fully employed elsewhere and only referee as a hobby. However, they get paid a retainer by the Irish Rugby Union to cover them for any income they might lose should they have to take time off from work, since such duties can entail absences of a few weeks at a time. In my case, though, being a fully professional referee makes life so much easier. It means that there is no pressure on me to rush from a daily job to referee, perhaps in another country, or to hurry home so that I can get back to work by a specific time.

When I was still employed as a technician I had a great understanding with the school concerning getting time off to referee. When the caretaker was on holiday or ill, or if there was a need to undertake some of his duties during the school day (since he didn't work between 9.30am and 3.30pm) I was the one called upon, for which I received no payment. This made sense, since I used to do that very job myself before becoming a technician. Yet there were certain aspects of it which weren't all that attractive, such as having to come in to school by 6.30 each morning. So, when I required time off to travel here and there in order to referee, there was no problem. In that respect I'm very grateful to many of the staff for their support, for example the headmaster, Arwyn Thomas and later, Iwan Rees. Also Dyfed Llywelyn, the head of technology and my line manager, who was very supportive when I required an occasional day off or needed to leave school early to get to a particular match in time. In addition Ieuan Morgan, the head of science who later became the deputy headmaster, took a great interest in my career as a referee and was very keen to see me make a success of it.

Turning professional gave me much more time to prepare physically for refereeing at the highest level. In the past I used to try and keep fit, usually after work, by running and regularly going to the gym. Now I have time to do all of that, and more, in a much more orderly and relaxed fashion. In addition, the two referees who are contracted centrally by the union attend special sessions at the Vale Hotel – the training HQ of the Wales rugby team – and in Cardiff, under the guidance of Huw Wiltshire, the WRU National Fitness Director, who looks after the fitness of the referees on the panel. Huw also prepares individual training programmes for each of us, which we can follow when we go to the gym on our own.

In the past keeping fit was a big problem for me. Rather, I should say that trying to regulate my weight was a nightmare which, of course, had a bearing on my fitness. When I was about twenty years old I weighed about sixteen stone. In fact I was fat and grossly overweight. I loved eating and would devour food at every opportunity. To make matters worse it wasn't healthy food either, for I lived on a diet of kebabs, chips and takeaways, which I consumed in great numbers. I decided that I would have to lose weight. I didn't like the way I looked and neither was I happy with the way in which I thought others saw me. Yet I wasn't prepared to go on a diet or to eat wisely, as most people do. I wanted to lose weight and lose it fast, but I wanted to carry on stuffing myself with as much food as possible. So I chose the most stupid method of all. When I felt that I was unable to deny myself the pleasure of having a bellyful of food, I would devour it avidly and then make myself ill so that I would vomit it up again. In other words I was suffering from bulimia, but at the time I wasn't prepared to admit to the harm it was doing to my constitution or my psychological state. I did lose about five stone in a matter of months, but I was now looking very pale and ill. I had also lost that sparkle that previously had made me a bubbly, popular character.

I battled with bulimia for years, although I didn't resort to making myself sick quite so often during the latter years of the illness. Yet I would still be tempted to do so from time to time, especially if I felt that I was eating too much or that I was putting on weight. Fortunately, I recently came to my senses due to circumstances that I wish had never come to pass, to

With my grandmother,
Maggie Moultan and
grandfather, Willy Moultan.
I miss them both terribly.

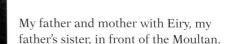

My father and mother with Eiry, my
father's sister, in front of the Moultan.

In the arms of my mum, a
wonderful person and the
best mum one could have
ever wished for. I miss her
so much and would do
anything to be able to be in
her arms right now.

My mother's parents, Lyn and Maud Nicholas.

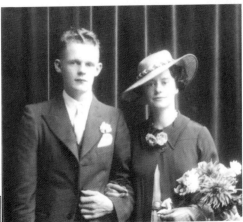

Me as a youngster with Fred on Bancyreos fields, where I spent a lot of time looking after the horses.

Ready for Sunday School – me and my cousin Helen, who lived next to us in Maeslan for years. We were like brother and sister.

Wasn't I a nice-looking lad? Wel, that's what my mother used to say.

I was a born referee, there's no doubt! I've got a whistle in my mouth for a bike race on the street in Maeslan. In the photo: Wynn Robinson, Mark Lloyd, Louise Robinson, Christopher Lloyd and Helen Owens.

Mynyddcerrig primary school. The whole school is in the picture, mind you, with Wyn Gravell, the headmaster, and Margaret Tunuchie, the teacher.

Mynyddcerrig club's trip to the seaside. I'd always wanted to be Tarzan!

Me, Uncle Ken and my father on holiday in north Wales. Uncle Ken was very good to me and and I really miss him.

Year 8, Maes yr Yrfa School. Many people think I look naughty – I don't think so!

Starting at Maes yr Yrfa School. Year 8 with the form teacher, Mr Wynford Nicholas.

Class 1B, Gwendraeth School.

Mynyddcerrig athletics team for Mynydd Mawr primary school sports day.

I won the pool tournament at Mynyddcerrig club at the tender age of 14. Mind you, everyone else was still drunk after New Year's Eve! I still play on New Year's Day unless there's a rugby match.

Playing the part of Idwal, one of Ifan Gruffydd's characters, at Mynyddcerrig School. It was easy to make people laugh by playing Idwal – his appearance was enough to pull the house down.

Me and my friend, Lyndon Davies. The two of us would frequently appear on stage at school mimicking teachers.

Mynyddcerrig pool team after winning the Cwm Gwendraeth Pool Cup. Back row: Kerry Prosser, Franco Saracinni, Martin Lewis. Front row: Len Jones, me, Robert Owen, Johny Wilcox, Graham Owen and Cecil Jones.

The Tir Garn family. I spent many years there as one of the family, enjoying farming every Saturday. Dilys, Dewi, Rhiannon, Angharad and Naomi at Mynyddcerrig carnival.

Members of Llanarthne Young Farmers. At each member's wedding, it was customary do dress like this – the happy couple would walk under the pitchforks as they left the chapel. In the photo: me, Bari Bron Berllan, Meirion Garnlwyd, Diane Bron Berllan, his sister Wendy, and Nia Roberts in the middle.

My last day in my room at Maes yr Yrfa School where I worked for almost 13 years.

The Science Department. Caryl, Bill and Sharon with me and Robert Samms, the caretaker. Memorable times.

Some of the comedians filming *Jocars*, the TV series, in Felin Fach.

My cousin Wyn's children, Dion (my godson) and his brother Dylan.

Cerys and Elis who often come round for tea. They're my cousin Wayne and his wife Julie's children.

With Ifan and Mared, my cousin Helen and her husband Gwyndaf's children.

I became good friends with several players that I'd refereed. Arwel Thomas was a great outside half, and we're still good friends to this day.

With some poor but happy and friendly people in Victoria, Zimbabwe. On my left is George, quite a character.

Running onto Stradey Park for the first time as a linesman in a League match between Llanelli and Bridgend.

Below: refing in the early days. Maesteg v Carmarthen Athletic.

Running the line at St Helens in the game between Swansea and Cardiff – I got a shock when Wales centre, Mike Hall, called me names that I can't repeat here!

A night to remember both on and off the field. Running the line with Mark
Sayers from Felinfoel and the unique Derek Bevan as referee for Ieuan Evans's
testimonial game, with Ken Parffit in the middle.

One of the first continental trips to Amsterdam, with Hugh Banfield and Nigel
Whitehouse.

A very proud day, and a photo displayed with pride and honour at home in Pontyberem and Mynyddcerrig. I've got Mam and Dad to thank for everything I've accomplished so far. I couldn't have wished for better nor for a different upbringing.

Sending one of Bourgoin's players to the sin bin in a Heineken Cup match in Bath. They didn't understand a word – but they understood the card!

Sending the giant Fabien Pelous to the sin bin in the final of the Heineken Cup at the Millennium Stadium in 2008.

Meeting Prince William before the Wales v Ireland match in 2007.

The twelve disciples – only the twelve best refs in the world were allowed to ref in the World Cup, 2007.

Me showing my cap in 2007 after the Union decided to award caps to international referees for the first time.

which I shall refer later. I continue to enjoy my food and I am now able to regulate my weight in ways which are much more acceptable. I have also been able to help others come to terms with this illness and to deal with its consequences, mainly by talking publicly about it at various events. One such event was a week-long programme at the National Assembly for Wales, specifically designed to draw attention to eating disorders.

Despite the apparent advantages of becoming a professional referee, there were many factors which initially prevented me from making a final decision. Firstly, I would certainly miss the camaraderie at Maes yr Yrfa. Secondly, I would now be doing something for a living which previously had been a leisure pursuit in my case, and I wasn't sure whether I would be able to cope with that. Thirdly, I have always hankered after stability and have been unwilling to see things change, even in a comparatively insignificant context. For example, whenever I decided to sell one of my cars, I would always be loathe to see it go when the time came. In the same way, moving from the area where I was brought up to go and live in somewhere like Cardiff would not appeal to me at all; although that might have been a wise move in many ways, especially since my work entails that I spend a lot of time there. In addition, the period when I 'came out' and announced that I was gay was a particularly difficult time for me and, in many respects, life then might well have been easier if I had moved to Cardiff. But I decided to stay in my native area and I have no regrets. By the same token I am now prepared to admit that the best decision I ever made was to become a professional rugby referee.

CHAPTER 6

Problems

NATURALLY MY PARENTS BECAME very alarmed when they found the note I'd left them in April 1996, during that most difficult of times for me, telling them that I was going to take my own life. They didn't know where to start looking for me, so they contacted the police and informed them of the note before setting out to try and find me at once. Apparently the area was awash with people and police with dogs trying to locate me, but to no avail. Eventually it was decided to get the police helicopter to assist with the search. A good few hours after I'd left the house, it spotted me lying on the top of Bancyddraenen Mountain.

I had walked for hours that morning, through the fields and over the mountains near my home where I had spent most of my childhood years. I was in a trance, trying to get my head around what was happening and visiting the places that meant something special to me for what appeared to be the last time. Sometime after I had lain down and taken the supposedly fatal overdose of tablets, I was spotted by the helicopter crew and airlifted to Glangwili Hospital in Carmarthen. It was thought at the time that I would have died had the crew taken just thirty minutes longer to find me. I also had a shotgun with me, and I'm sure that if I had not taken the overdose I would have probably pulled the trigger. Strangely, therefore, the overdose I took actually saved me in the end. Recently, the officer who had lifted me off the mountain introduced himself to me. I thanked him for what he'd done but I was none the wiser for seeing him, since to this day I have no recollection at all of being rescued.

I was in hospital for four days – long enough for me to take stock of what had happened and to realise how stupidly I had behaved. I felt so ashamed and embarrassed about what I had done; for putting my mum and dad through hell and, of course, for all the trouble that people had taken to try and find me – not least the police. There were also implications with regard to the cost of police resources and the time they had spent looking for me. I can only apologise from the bottom of my heart for all of that. During that period friends and family members called regularly to see me, day and night. Although I felt so guilty for what I had done, I was very glad of their company and thankful for the support they gave my parents at a very difficult time. I am greatly indebted to them all.

I had realised by then how dangerous taking steroids could be, and also that I had dabbled with them for the very last time. Yet the steroids alone were not responsible for getting me into such a state. In fact, they constituted just a small part of the problem. The main reason for my being so depressed and wanting to take my own life was the fact that I was gay and that, although I didn't want to be gay, there was nothing I could do about it. But I couldn't begin to recognise the extent of the mental torture that I'd put my parents through and I felt so sorry for the grief I had caused them. I was also so ashamed that I had tried to deal with my problems in such an extreme and inconsiderate manner, although, at the time, I didn't think that there was any other option open to me. But that hideous experience made me appreciate the value of life and the importance of friends and family. Ultimately the incident made me more resilient and better equipped to deal with the all-important decision that I would take some years later, namely to 'come out' and announce that I was gay.

Ironically, after leaving Glangwili, I obtained an acting part in two episodes of *Pobol y Cwm*, playing a faith healer. At that time I could have done with the assistance of such a character myself! Some three weeks later I was the compere at a concert held in Newquay in Cardiganshire, which put me under some strain but also provided some form of therapy. In addition I had been diagnosed as suffering from colitis which, according to the doctors, was largely the result of the mental strain I had been under in recent years. I still suffer from that particular ailment but I'm able to control it fairly successfully. Although there is medication available to keep it in check, I find I don't need it these days since the condition seems to have stabilised. It flares up every so often but I'm able to carry on without any major disruption. My only worry is that when it strikes, which can happen suddenly and with little warning, I have to go to the toilet at once. On many occasions when out running, I have had to jump over a hedge or run into a nearby wood. One time I was shouted at and pursued by a local farmer who must have wondered what the hell I was doing in his field. Of course, I didn't hang about to explain the nature of my illness to him. The condition could cause even more embarrassment if I happened to be refereeing an important match at the time, particularly if it was being televised live. Fortunately this hasn't happened... yet!

It is commonly thought that gay men worry more about their appearance than others. Perhaps that explains why I became obsessed with 'looking good'. As I have already mentioned, keeping my weight under control had been a great problem for me over the years and I had found that one answer, to my stupid way of thinking, was to make myself ill after eating. I also began to do some weightlifting in order to try and build some muscle, in the small multi-gym at Maes yr Yrfa. I would go there some three evenings a week along with one of the teachers, Gwynallt Price, who was a keep-fit enthusiast, despite being in his fifties by then. He was one of the 'old school' and, although he never actually taught me, he was a senior staff member to whom I was sent on a few occasions when I had been misbehaving in class. But he was a fair and kind man and I had a lot of respect for him, both as a pupil and a fellow staff member.

One evening when I was on the weights in the gym, Terry Davies came in to pick up his son, Steven (a friend of mine), after rugby training. We got talking and he told me about a gym in the neighbouring village of Cross Hands which had excellent keep-fit facilities. It was run by Gareth Zags Isaacs and Dorian Price, a former local rugby player and an ex-coach of Cefneithin Rugby Club. There they would offer help to any newcomers and show them how to do weight training properly. From then on, along with Zags, Andrew Sainty, Peter Watts, Joni Simons and Arwyn Peng Edwards, I would train there almost every night and before long I was looking leaner and fitter. However, after a while, I wanted to be in even better shape and more muscular in my appearance. After talking to someone whom I knew was taking steroid tablets, I came to believe that they could give me the type of body that I wanted. Before long I was taking them myself. Some of the lads who were used to them had warned me that the safest way was to take them for a while, then break off for a period before starting again. However, since I liked my new physique so much, I was stupid enough to think that I had no need to lay off them even for a short period and that I could just keep taking more and more. In addition, I started to use liquid steroids and to inject myself, which was, in itself, a very dangerous practice. As a result, during the five years I was on steroids, I suffered some bad side effects. I was admitted to hospital on three occasions to remove a lump from my chest. I was also short-tempered, became tired quickly and suffered from insomnia. Neither was I as fit as I should have been, since, by this time, I weighed 15 stone; not because I was fat but because I carried so much muscle. Yet I was still unhappy with the person I was. After so many years of taking steroids I became depressed, which is one of the most harmful side effects. That's how I came to the conclusion that committing suicide would provide a way out. But, of course, that other important issue had also been weighing heavily on my mind.

Ever since I was 17 or 18 years old I'd known that there was something different about me in comparison with most other boys. I fancied girls at that time and would go on dates with them on a regular basis. I went out with one particular girl for about a year and a half. Although she was a lovely and very attractive person, I knew that things weren't quite right between us and that I was basically unhappy with our relationship. Not because I didn't love her or fancy her – I did very much – but because I was having these strange feelings that I could not control. When I was 19 years old I went with another gay lad for the very first time and, although I felt the experience was pleasant and natural at the time, the fact that I had been with him later left me full of remorse and scared. So I didn't go with another boy for a few years after that. In the meantime I continued to date girls, regardless of the fact that, deep down, I still had this longing to meet boys. However, as time went by, dating girls began to feel more and more unnatural. But I didn't want to be as I was and I even made an appointment with my doctor at Tumble surgery to see if there was anything I could do to get rid of this attraction I had for men. I was getting so depressed that I even asked him if I could have a chemical castration to stop me from being gay. I had heard or read somewhere that this was possible.

But it's not so easy to change who you are. In fact, when it's a matter of being attracted to men or women, I don't think you have a choice. I decided to do something about the fact that I wanted relationships with boys; but that happened by accident. I had gone to Swansea with friends for the annual Young Farmers' Grand Dance and during the evening I happened to be with a group who were discussing how a few of the lads had got lost in the city the previous year. They had apparently asked some locals for directions to the dance, which was being held at Jumping Jacks on the Kingsway. But, as a joke, they were sent to a club in the area which was very popular with the gay community. I asked what the club was called, whilst at the same time trying to look disinterested and innocent, and got a reply. The next time we visited Swansea, I deliberately lost my friends to give me the opportunity to look for Champers, the gay club in question.

Walking in on my own, with everyone seemingly staring at me, was a very strange and frightening experience. Not knowing what to do or say, I walked up to the bar and ordered a drink. Before long several people had come up to talk to me and most of them were very friendly. In fact I made some good friends that night and have kept in touch with them ever since. I enjoyed my visit to Champers, but I still had the strange old feeling that something wasn't right. I then moved on, with the few friends that I had made that night, to a gay nightclub just up the road called the Palace. I arrived home that night feeling that I had taken a very positive step with regard to being honest about the fact that I was gay. Yet when my friends asked what had happened to me that night, I replied that I'd got off with a girl from the Townhill area that I'd happened to meet and had gone back to her place.

That's how it was for many years: living a lie. I returned to the gay club on more than one occasion but I still didn't want anybody to know about me, apart from one person. When I was about 22, I told a girl who was one of my closest friends that I was gay. I asked her to keep it a secret and she didn't breathe a word to anyone.

The most difficult aspect for me to deal with at the time was that I didn't want to carry on in that way, or to be that way inclined. I hated having such feelings yet there was nothing I could do about them, although I'd tried hard to forget about them in the hope that they would go away. I remember going to a gay club one night and almost immediately noticing a chap whom I recognised, knowing full well that he would also recognise me. I was so terrified that he would see me and possibly tell other people about it that I shot out of the club at speed, despite the fact that I'd paid £6 to get in only ten minutes previously! I later came to learn that gay people never tend to 'out' other gays or bisexual guys who are 'in the closet' or to reveal whom they might have seen in a gay club, which was a great relief.

During the next eight years or so I had several gay relationships, one which lasted twelve months even, but they never seemed to work out in the end. The main reason was that I was so terrified of being seen in the company of another man. Perhaps things are different in this day and age. The internet, and the fact that society today is more prepared to recognise gay relationships, makes it easier for people to 'come out'. Some fifteen years ago, when I began to have doubts concerning my sexuality, nobody in Mynyddcerrig would tolerate seeing two lads walking around the village in a gay relationship. The tendency in those days was to think that gay men were only to be found in places such as ladies fashion shops and hairdressing salons, or serving meals on airplanes. Indeed, I often walked past salons and looked furtively inside to see if I could get some idea of how a gay man would look.

The fact that I couldn't be open about the relationships I had with other men was rather sad in some ways. In others, it led to many an amusing incident. I remember going to the Pizza Hut in Swansea with a guy I had met on an internet chat room. Who should come in but Dwayne Peel, an old friend of mine, and Jessica, his girlfriend. I told my date to make a run for the toilet before they spotted us, while I shot off to pay at the till, although we hadn't yet been served. I had a brief word with the young couple whilst waiting for my pizza, which was now going to be a take away and would be eaten in the car instead of in the warmth and relative comfort of Pizza Hut. I don't know whether Dwayne suspected anything; I never asked him and he has never mentioned that particular night to me. However, one thing was certain: after such a pantomime I could hardly expect the guy I was dating to want to continue in that fashion or meet up again. After all, being asked to hide in the toilets for ten minutes and then having to eat his pizza in a car park on the Kingsway in Swansea doesn't make for a pleasant night out! That was the case with several other dates and relationships I entered into over the years. All of this weighed heavily on my mind and contributed to that foolish thought on top of Bancyddraenen Mountain that there was only one feasible answer to all my problems. Fortunately, some years later, I became better equipped to deal publicly with the fact that I was gay.

Things have changed. I was recently with the same partner for about three years, but this relationship unfortunately came to an end in 2008. I met Dan when I was out in Cardiff on the night of the Wales v Scotland game and, although it wasn't an easy relationship, mainly because my career took me away from home so often, there were some great times during those three years and I don't regret any of it. Unlike many gay people, I don't tend to have a particularly gay lifestyle. Not that there is anything wrong with that, but I live my life as I would if I were a straight person. After all, I am just a normal guy who happens to be gay; yet I could never have imagined ten years ago that such a situation would be possible.

After years of denial and concealment I came to the conclusion, when I was 32 years old, that I needed to be open concerning my sexuality. All the deceit was having an effect on my personality. When refereeing away from home, although I'd perform my duties creditably, I was always conscious of the fact that there seemed to be an added burden upon my shoulders. Many of the international referees I socialise with tell me that these days I'm a completely different person, in that I appear happier and more content and that I'm much more affable in company. I confess that, in the past, I used to feel rather apprehensive when mixing with them socially, in case it became apparent that I was gay.

Recently I accepted an invitation to become an ambassador for the Wales Centre for Excellence support line for gay people

– a charity based in Swansea. Part of my role is to visit schools and share some of my experiences of being gay and coming out. I am always prepared to speak, either in public or in private with individuals, if it appears that what I have to say could be a comfort or of assistance. One of the most important messages I try to get across is that in order for you to do well in school and in life you must be happy with yourself, otherwise you cannot fulfil your true potential no matter what field of work or sport you choose. This was a lesson I learned the hard way.

One incident in particular, which occurred during the period we were filming the second series of ex-rugby star Jonathan Davies' talkshow on S4C, prompted me to 'come out'. I was in McDonald's in Carmarthen when a crowd of schoolchildren came in. When they saw me, they all began to sing the tune which led into a particular item on the *Jonathan* show, and they were obviously having a lot of fun doing so. Many of them came over to ask for my autograph, which made me realise that they took me to be some kind of celebrity whom they could look up to. I, on the other hand, knew that I was living a lie, which made me feel unworthy of being a role model for them. Soon after that incident I decided that 'coming out' and putting the record straight regarding my sexual orientation was preferable to having people find out through stories in the tabloid press. It wasn't my intention to wave the flag on behalf of the gay community, as it were, but rather just to be honest.

My first task was to tell my mother. Although it was a difficult and tearful experience for both of us, and although she confessed to feeling a little disappointed, she told me that the news hadn't been entirely unexpected and that she'd had her suspicions that I might be gay, having found some gay magazines under my bed a few years previously. She also told me that it was important for me to realise that it wouldn't have any bearing on the relationship that existed between us. She would continue to love me as any mother would love her son. I was comforted by the way in which she had reacted but I knew that telling my father would be much more difficult and it was an experience I wasn't prepared to face. So I asked my mother to break it to him, which she did some two weeks later.

He was quite upset on hearing the news and remained so for about a month. He continued to talk to me but it was as if he didn't know what to say. The word 'gay' isn't in his vocabulary and to this day he's never mentioned it to me. He has this dated idea that the 'camp' characters on television, such as Shaun in *Coronation Street*, are the gay people of this world and he has little regard for them. We are still great friends and he comes with me occasionally to rugby matches. But he says some things which seem to suggest that he doesn't realise, or possibly doesn't wish to recognise, the significance of the fact that I've 'come out'. Not so long ago I was sitting with him at a game when he drew my attention to a smart young girl nearby. 'Look at that young lady there,' he said, 'isn't she pretty! Why don't you think about taking her as your wife?'

I will never forget the day when my cousins (Wynn, Adrian, Kevin and Wayne) and I were all seated around the table at my house, having tea after a long day's biking. I was about ten years old at the time and Adrian, who was about three years older, prompted me to ask my father what a 'homo' (i.e. homosexual) was. I had no idea what it meant and nor did my father. When I asked him, he replied innocently and quite sincerely, 'I don't know, you'd better ask your mother. I think it is a type of washing powder.' In fact he was right, but that wasn't what my cousins thought and they were right too!

After telling my mother on the Thursday that I was gay, I telephoned Robert Yeman, the WRU referees manager, to ask if I could come and see him. That particular evening he and his wife Christine had arranged to go out for a meal on the occasion of their wedding anniversary. When Christine heard Robert's reaction on the phone, she sensed that something was up and insisted that they cancel the restaurant reservation so that I could go to see them. I'm very grateful to them for that favour and for all the support they've shown me over the years. Robert has been a good friend as well as a conscientious and efficient boss, despite the fact that I have probably put his patience to the test on several occasions.

I wanted to know whether the fact that I was intending to 'come out' was likely to have a bearing on my career as a referee – particularly with regard to my dealings with players and coaches. In Robert's opinion it wouldn't make any difference at all, but he mentioned that he would, as a matter of course, inform the senior officials of the WRU at the time, namely, Steve Lewis, David Moffett and David Pickering. Their reaction was the same as Robert's and I am so grateful to them for their support, and for the continuing support of Roger Lewis and the Welsh Rugby Union today. If I had had to make the choice between living a lie in order to continue with my refereeing career and giving it up in order to try and be happy in my life, then I really don't know what decision I would have made.

The next step was to send text messages on the Saturday to all my friends living locally: Wayne Thomas, Hefin Death, Gari Cute, Matthew Rowe, Baker, Kelvin, Justin Lloyd, Slugs, Craig Bonnell, Richard Babs, Baglin, Joni Clayton, Richard Hardy, Dorian, Willis and Pete Pig as well as some of my cousins and their wives. I got a reply from all of them except one old school friend who used to play in the same rugby team as me. I still see him occasionally and there has been no change in our relationship; yet he has never admitted to receiving that text message from me.

Most of them rang me as soon as they got the text to see if I was OK. A few wanted to know if it was true or whether I was just winding them up. But they all stressed that it would make no difference to their relationship with me and that, as far as they were concerned, our friendship would be just as strong as it had always been. And they were right. Regardless of how difficult it had been to 'come out', knowing that my old circle of friends was still there for me was a great comfort. I'm very grateful also to my relatives for their support during that difficult period and for the support they gave my parents. It was a particularly trying time and I wouldn't have been able to get through it without the assistance of friends and family. I am greatly in their debt.

Having their support is the reason I decided to stay in my native area rather than going to live in Cardiff, say, where people would take little notice of the fact that I was gay and where I wouldn't be recognised by many. Perhaps things might be different these days since more people know of me. I do seem to get recognised wherever I go now, but that is no doubt due to being known as 'the gay referee' and to my media work. But I have always been attached to my own locality and I would never want to move away. Well, not at the moment anyway, as I have no reason to do so, and my local community, family and friends mean so much to me. But I suppose one should never say 'never'!

It's great to be able to mingle with celebrities from the world of rugby on every continent but it's always nice to come home to the 'real world' of my native area, where I am 'Nigel' to all and sundry and where I am no different to anyone else. My friends and social circle are the same now as they were years ago, whereas had I 'come out' when I was sixteen years old it's possible that I would have completely different acquaintances. I would then, perhaps, have had to turn to a group of girls or other gay lads for company, although I have very good female friends such as Julie, the wife of my cousin, Wayne Nichols, and Melanie Jenkins, who does most of my ironing for me. (Although I do most of the house chores myself, ironing is the one thing I hate doing.)

After 'coming out' most people were very supportive towards me and they would stop for a chat when we met on the street, for example and they continue to do so. In fact nothing has changed. I am the same Nigel Owens today as ever before, apart from the fact that people now know, of course, that I am gay. Yet there were a few who would seem uncomfortable in my company or when I would bump into them on the street. In the beginning, that got me down, but by now, however, it doesn't bother me as my true friends are still my friends and always will be. I was also aware that I was the subject of a lot of gossip, much of which was the product of vivid imaginations as opposed to any substance. I much prefer people who are prepared to confront me face to face than those who gossip behind my back, yet are so pleasant and polite to my face.

I also sent text messages to my three fellow presenters on the TV programme *Jonathan* and got the same positive response. Indeed, Jonathan Davies telephoned me to say, 'I don't care if you're bonking cows, we will still be friends!' The three of them were very supportive, particularly Eleri Siôn who has since gone out with me as a companion on a few occasions. One night we ended up in Pulse, a gay bar in Cardiff, and had a great time. The fact that I had come out enabled the scriptwriters to include an abundance of suggestive cracks to be used by Rowland Phillips and the other two. Nevertheless it was obvious that some viewers thought that all these references to my being gay were part of a huge joke because one person recently asked me, in all seriousness, whether Eleri Siôn and I were an item!

On the Sunday I telephoned Huw Watkins, one of my best friends and a fellow referee, to tell him my news. The following day he received an email from New Zealand, in which our good friend Bryce Lawrence asked if the story that I was gay was true. I was expecting the telephone lines in Pontyberem to be buzzing that weekend but I was amazed that the news had got as far as the southern hemisphere. Also that Monday I was working out at my usual fitness centre when Barrie Williams, the international hooker and then captain of the Ospreys, came up to me and shook my hand. He told me that he thought I had been very brave and wanted me to know that my announcement would not make any difference to him or to his fellow players. I got the same response from Gethin Jenkins of the Cardiff Blues when I travelled back on the same plane as them from Ireland, having refereed their match against Connacht.

I'm pleased to say that to this day I've not heard one malicious comment from any players or officials in the rugby world concerning the fact that I'm gay. Although I was told by a colleague that one or two referees had said to Robert Yeman that they did not want to travel away with me as fellow officials when I was refereeing. I don't know whether this is true, nor have I bothered to ask. I don't have a problem at all with anyone not wishing to be in my company if they do not feel comfortable with the situation. But I would like to think that they would be men enough to tell me so to my face and not talk behind my back in the hope that their identity would not be known. If they were that kind of person then I would not, in any event, wish them to be part of my officiating team.

I tend to get on well with players off the field and there's been absolutely no difference in the way they've responded to me since I've 'come out'. In fact I am very good friends with some of the Welsh team players, and following the Ireland v Wales Grand Slam match in Cardiff in 2008, a few of them and their wives and girlfriends came with me to Club X (after the bars had closed in Tiger Tiger and Oceana) and we had a great night. Yet I wouldn't be surprised if some of them were to feel uncomfortable if just two of us were seen together, however innocuous the circumstances, since gossip can grow from nothing. I spoke recently to a Welshman who was playing for Doncaster and he asked me if it was true that I was going out with a member of the Welsh rugby team. This story was frequently heard at the time in English rugby circles. At the end of last season I was asked the same question by one or two of the England players whilst having a few beers with them after an international match in Manchester. Danny Care, the England scrum-half, was convinced it was true. It took me a while to persuade him that it was just a stupid rumour. The story, of course, is completely unfounded and although it doesn't bother me, for I expect that kind of tale to rear its head from time to time, I feel sorry for the player concerned since it's a fact that he's not gay.

Sometime after I'd 'come out' I was refereeing the Blues against the Scarlets at the Arms Park. Since it was a mid-week match in September, two friends from Pontyberem, Owain Baglin and Christian Lewis (who is known as 'Baker' in the village), came with me to the game. I telephoned Vicky in the Blues office, who's always ready to help, to get them tickets. Unfortunately the machine which printed the tickets wasn't working so she told me that she'd have a word with the steward in order to reserve two seats for them in the Committee Box.

As I warmed up before kick-off the two of them were enjoying a pint in front of the stand whilst shouting an occasional derogatory remark in my direction. As I made my way back to the changing room they asked me where they'd be sitting. I told them that I'd be giving their names to the steward and that he would direct them to their seats. The steward was a huge chap, about 6ft 6ins tall, and I told him, 'My mate and his boyfriend will be with you soon. Could you show them to their seats, please?' I should emphasise that the two of them are completely straight and are married now. But, full of bravado, they went up to the steward and said, 'The Ref told us to come and see you so that you could take us to our seats.' And that's what happened. But as they sat down he turned to them, saying, 'You know, you don't look it. I would never have guessed.'

'Guessed what?' they asked.

'Well, you know,' he said.

'No, we don't. What are you on about?'

'Oh, never mind,' he said, and walked away.

I didn't mention the matter to the boys on the journey

home but they were still obviously very puzzled as to what the steward had meant. On the Saturday night, back in the village rugby club, I told the tale in full and added, 'That'll teach you not to shout nasty remarks at the referee!' Of course the story went down really well with the other lads in the club.

What surprised me more than anything was that the media had ignored the fact that I'd come out until about fifteen months later. At that point, before the 2007 World Cup, I did an interview for the BBC Radio Wales programme *Scrum V* on the subject of being gay in the macho world of rugby. Prior to that I hadn't spoken publicly on the matter because Robert Yeman wished to protect me from any possible negative comments by the press, fearing that they might have a detrimental effect on my performances as a referee. By that time I had been informed that I would be taking charge of the Bledisloe Cup match between Australia and New Zealand and that I would be one of the referees officiating at the World Cup.

Following that radio interview the *Wales on Sunday* newspaper ran the story with a very positive slant, I must say. Yet they claimed that they'd actually spoken to me, which wasn't true – they'd lifted the story in its entirety from the radio programme. It was then picked up by a number of other publications, which varied from the *Sun* to the local *Carmarthen Journal* which gave it front page coverage. What worried me most of all was that my parents, once again, would be reading some of these reports and would almost certainly be upset by them. For, as a family, we'd thought that we had dealt with the matter once and for all, but there it was back in the news. I gave a lot of thought, therefore, as to whether I should write this autobiography (and the prior Welsh version) or not. I certainly didn't wish to cause my parents any further worry and neither was I sure whether I wanted my private life to be put under the microscope. Yet I didn't want others to suffer the same problems that affected me and I knew that there were people who could benefit from my experiences should they be faced with similar circumstances. So I decided to tell my story, realising full well that in doing so I had to be completely honest.

I tried to explain to my parents that while I was a public figure we would unfortunately have to accept sensationalist publicity in the press and that there was very little I could do about it. I don't wish to hide behind the problems that I've had; rather, I hope that I can use my status as a public figure to help others who are trying to come to terms with similar difficulties.

I recently received an email from a young lad who was gay but didn't know how to tell his parents. In the past they had tended to mock gay people, but by watching television programmes such as *Jonathan* and *Noson Lawen* they had become fans of mine and had come to accept that being gay was not something to be condemned. Their son had even heard them tell friends who were over for dinner, 'Well, it must be ok to be gay if Nigel Owens is.' As a result, that particular lad found it easier to tell his parents that he was gay and to get them to accept that fact. I was glad to hear that I had been able to help.

In fact I received some very nice letters and a few heartfelt 'thank you' messages in my Facebook inbox after the publication of the Welsh version of this book and also following the appearance of extracts from the book in the press. One touching message was from a woman who thanked me so much for helping her son come to terms with being gay. A few months before the story of my 'coming out' and attempted suicide appeared in the press, her sixteen-year-old son had tried to kill himself. Like me, he had been very lucky and got a second chance. It was only after reading about my experiences in the press that he decided to pluck up the courage to tell his parents why he had tried to take his own life. His mother wrote to me and said, 'I thank you from the bottom of my heart. After reading extracts of your book on the internet and papers my son has come to realise that there's nothing wrong with being gay, and thanks to role models like you we've realised we can get on with life and be a family again, and my son now can accept who he is and knows that we still love him no matter what.' This really brought the memories flooding back, reminding me how difficult coming to terms with being gay can be, not just for individuals but also for families.

While I was refereeing in the World Cup, *The Times* published a full-page article, which I had previously approved, the day before I was to take charge of my first game. It was a very positive take on the fact that I was the first gay person to 'come out' in professional rugby circles. A few days later I received a telephone call from Rob Hayward, a former Member of Parliament in the Bristol area, informing me that I had been nominated by him and others for the Stonewall Sports Personality Award and that I might be required to go to London for the awards ceremony. Stonewall is a body which does commendable work on behalf of gay people, so I accepted the invitation. Therefore, after returning from the World Cup, off I went to London.

I must confess that I was shocked to learn that I had won the award. The reasons for this achievement, I understand, were that I had 'come out' in the very macho world of rugby, that I was very proud of the person that I was and that I had shown the way forward to others like myself who were at the very highest level of achievement in the sporting world. Yet when I 'came out' it hadn't been my intention to raise the profile of gay people or to fight any battles, however worthy they might have been. But I'm very proud of that award and of the honour which comes with it, as well as being glad to draw attention to some of the difficulties that gay people have to face on a daily basis. I have attended a few functions for Stonewall Wales as a guest speaker to talk of my experiences, which I hope have helped to raise awareness of the many issues that face young gay people today.

Being gay has its problems. I'm very glad that I came to terms with my sexuality before getting into a heterosexual relationship with which I didn't feel comfortable and which might have led to my getting married and having children. That could have resulted in my having to turn my back on my family, or live a double life for the rest of my life, which has happened to many gay men, as I would have been eventually forced to admit that I could only be happy with another male for a partner. That would obviously lead to a great deal of heartache for a number of people. On the other hand, it's possible that some children would be better off if they were brought up by gay parents who loved them and raised them as part of a secure and supportive family, rather than remaining with their natural parents if they are unfit to have children. This is not an argument I would want to get into, as I can see the pros and cons on the both sides, maybe this comes from the fact that I am a referee and have to be neutral and fair all the time, although I do have my own personal views on it.

I think it is very important that every child is brought up by both parents together, whenever possible, so I have to accept that I will probably never have children myself. That bothers me, for I would be delighted to have children of my own. I could then share my life with them and still enjoy the experience of having my own family after both my parents had passed away. However, I am blessed with a very close family. I am godfather to two children: Dion (the son of my cousin, Wynn Robinson and his wife Kay) and Ffion Haf (the daughter of one of my closest friends, Joni Clayton and his wife Elen). No one has any idea of how pleased I was to be given that duty and honour. I must confess that both occasions gave rise to a few tears of happiness. Yet my family and friends would be the first to admit that having one's own little family is something else again.

I lead a very busy life and tend to fill the days and nights by keeping fit, refereeing, undertaking other rugby duties and fulfilling various engagements as an after-dinner speaker or entertainer. Contrary to the impression I might give on the rugby field or as a comedian, I enjoy spending time alone at home where I can relax in peace. However, one reason for my tendency to keep myself occupied is that being by myself can lead me to dwell on what I am missing by not having a family of my own. Although I am happy with my life, I do often wonder what it would be like to have children to care for and a wife to love. When I go to bed at night and turn out the light, my life sometimes seems quite empty. That sometimes makes me feel lonely and sad, and, if I am totally honest, perhaps a little scared as well. That's why I appreciate being in the company of friends and relatives and in particular their children when I get a chance to see them. I really enjoy taking Cerys and Elis, the children of Wayne and Julie, for a meal at McDonald's or on a visit to Joe's Ice Cream Parlour. Sometimes they call to have tea with me on their way home from school, along with Dion and his brother Dylan. I always love seeing them, along with my god-daughter Ffion.

Even though I was much more content after 'coming out' and giving up steroids, I had to continue my battle with bulimia for a long time. When out with friends it would be fairly easy for me to occasionally disappear in order to make myself throw up. I was able to make the excuse that my colitis complaint caused me to go to the toilet often and suddenly. But early in 2008 something happened which knocked me for six and completely changed my outlook on life: we were told that my mother had cancer. She'd gone for tests at the hospital, believing that the pain she'd been having was being caused by gallstones. Then we had confirmation of what had been troubling her. She was told after the initial tests that she had cancer of the lungs, stomach and liver and that she had only some nine months to live – even if she were to undergo treatment. A few days before she broke the news to my father and me, Uncle Ken died suddenly. The family hadn't seen him for a couple of days which was very unusual. When Emrys (another of my father's brothers) and I broke in to Ken's house with the help of a policeman, we found him lying on the bathroom floor. I took it badly, since Ken had been one of the great influences on my life and someone for whom I had great affection.

Two days later I was due to referee Wasps against Munster in a match which would determine which of the teams would go through to the Heineken Cup quarter-finals. I didn't fancy going to Limerick at all under the circumstances, but my parents persuaded me by convincing me that it would have been Ken's wish. I wore a black arm band in his memory that afternoon. With the support of Nigel Whitehouse and Huw Watkins, the two touch judges, and Derek Bevan, the video referee, I had a good game and received considerable praise from the French assessor, Joel Dume, who had no idea of the pressure I felt that afternoon. I have had great support from Whitehouse, Watkins, and Bevan on many difficult occasions during the last few seasons. In fact I don't think I could have got through some of those biggest matches without their friendship. I have been very lucky with regard to the officials I have had to work with, especially on the European weekends. I have also had valuable support from Jon Mason, Tim Hayes, Barrie Gregory, Neil Ballard and many others over the years, for which I am truly grateful.

Lawrence Dallaglio, the Wasps captain and Ian McGeechan, their coach, tried to say in a post-match interview that it was my fault that they lost that match. I wonder whether they would have said that had they known what I had gone through during the days leading up to the game? However, it has to be said that I was there to do my job as a professional referee whatever my personal problems were, and I was expected to perform my duties properly since there is 'no sentiment in sport'. Fair play to Dewi Morris, who was one of Sky's pundits for the game, for saying unequivocally that it was a case of sour grapes on Dallaglio's part and that he was just looking for excuses. In his opinion I had refereed very well, an observation which gave me considerable comfort during a very difficult time.

A few weeks later I was refereeing Wasps once again in their game against Leicester in the EDF semi-final. When I went into the Wasps changing room to do the usual pre-match duties, Lawrence came up to me and said that, after reviewing the video of the previous match, he was of the opinion that I had been right with regard to some decisions which he had originally questioned. After adding that he also thought that the yellow card I had given him had been fully deserved, he duly apologised. I was quite prepared to accept the apology, of course, but unfortunately I was the only person, apart from my touch judges, who could bear witness to it! Dallaglio's original claims had been very public, yet we referees have no means of publicly justifying decisions or of demonstrating that some critics have been unfair in condemning us.

For the next few days after the Wasps v Munster match I didn't know what to do. After returning from Ireland went straight to my parents' house as my mother was now out of hospital and home recovering, well that's what I thought and hoped. But my father and I were in for the biggest shock of our lives when she sat us both down to tell us this life changing news that hit us both for six. I spent the next few days at my parents' house, during which the implication of what my mother had told us began to hit home. I felt as if I'd run into a brick wall, but with the help of family members we gradually began to accept what lay ahead. However, in the light of what my mother was going through, how could I justify the problems I had been creating for myself for years in order to ensure that my appearance was acceptable? How could I continue to guzzle food and then make myself sick while my mother, and many others like her, were fighting for their lives because they were suffering from illnesses they could do nothing about? That was when

I decided that bulimia would never again have a hold on me. Since then I have never had the urge to regurgitate food. After all, doing so for the previous ten years had not improved my sad situation.

My attitude towards life and refereeing also changed during that time. There are some referees who get really worked up and worried about their performances on the field, particularly if they miss an offside or a knock-on. Of course I hope that I don't miss anything of note but I accept, nevertheless, that I'm bound to do so at times. If I fail to spot certain infringements from time to time, my reaction these days is not to dwell on it too much – as long as I've tried my best out there on the field one has to realise that there are some things in life which are much more important, notwithstanding the fact that I am always keen to give of my best as a referee, of course, and that I also want to be the best at what I do. In my opinion, such an attitude has helped me to give commendable performances on the field in very difficult circumstances.

I also began to look at my mother's illness in a more positive way. I had already reached the age of 36 and had been blessed with her love and presence for a longer period than that experienced by so many other children. Indeed, some children are denied that pleasure entirely. For a time there was more encouraging news. The cancer was thought to have started in the stomach rather than the lungs, which would, with a little luck, react better to treatment – although we still knew it was only a matter of time. I will never forget going with my mother and her sister Petula to meet the consultant at Glangwili Hospital. My father stayed at home, for he was finding it very difficult to cope with my mother's illness and would cry whenever we mentioned it. The doctor told us that with treatment, my mother could survive for about twelve months. Without it she would live a few months less. I broke down in tears at this point and so did Petula. My mother was very brave and said she didn't mind us crying but it would have to stop. She asked the doctor whether it would be worth her having any treatment at all, because she didn't want to have a poor quality of life for the remainder of her days just so that she could live for a few months longer.

It was something my mother and I would discuss later and at length at home. We came to the conclusion that she should give the treatment a go, to see how it progressed. We didn't really tell my father the details and implications of what we had been told at the hospital, for he preferred not to know and, in any event, it would have been too much for him to bear. But he knew that my mum was ill and that it would only be a matter of time before we would lose her. The priority for us at that stage was to spend as much time as we possibly could together as a family.

CHAPTER 7

Moving On

THERE IS A TENDENCY to think that since I now referee at the highest level, my job is that much more difficult. It's true that the pressure and tension which form an integral part of internationals or big Heineken Cup matches leave me feeling very tired, both mentally and physically. Games which are televised live and played in front of huge crowds can also leave me feeling rather exhausted. As a referee I have to make important decisions which can have a crucial effect on the result and can lead to a club making a profit or loss of many thousands of pounds. Winning or losing these days can have far-reaching consequences. I have just one opportunity to see what takes place on the field of play, and perhaps just one second to make an all-important decision. Of course, since so many television cameras are deployed these days, commentary teams, viewers at home and coaches with monitors at their disposal are all able to see particular incidents many times and can benefit from slow motion to examine pictures in detail before coming to a decision. Even then, their decisions are not always correct, take my word!

In order that I might make the right decisions it's important that I try to keep up with play, which means that I must be physically fit. But it is also vital to be mentally sharp. There are many young and very fit referees about these days, but unless you know what to do when you get to the breakdown, for example, then there is not much point getting there. Games at the highest level are much faster, yet the work of the referee in local district matches and the lower divisions of the union can be just as difficult, in different ways. In such matches the referee is usually on his own, without the assistance of neutral assistant referees or any technical aids, apart from a watch and a whistle. The fact that some players at that level lack a healthy attitude towards the game can also cause problems. This is particularly true of the lower levels and youth rugby.

In that respect I remember learning an important lesson some five years ago, despite the fact that I was already an experienced referee. I was in charge of an Under-16 match between Pontyberem and Betws. I live only a stone's throw away from the rugby field in Pontyberem Park and I like to help out my local club as much as possible. I don't think I was treating the match seriously enough or I certainly wasn't switched on to it as I would normally be when I referee some of the world's biggest matches, so I lost control to such an extent that I had to cut it short by about ten minutes. By that time everybody was fighting: the players, the replacements and some of the crowd. I had mistakenly gone into the game with the intention of allowing play to flow at every opportunity, since it was a youth match, and ignoring some offences which I would have penalised at a higher level. I learned, following that day, that I should always treat every match in the same way. After all, this would be the highest level of rugby some of those players would reach, so for them it was like playing for their country. I, however, had reacted in a manner that suggested that I was too important for a game at that level. In my defence, it should be remembered that in such games there are also some players who don't really want to be on the field. They're playing because of pressure from their parents, because all their mates are playing, or perhaps because they see such an occasion as a convenient opportunity to socialise in the club after the game. It follows that such people don't have the same respect for the laws of rugby, for other players or referees, and as a result their lack of discipline on the pitch can cause problems.

As a referee I have never found it difficult to deal with

indiscipline, since union guidelines state quite clearly which offences call for a red card. As a result, a kind of automatic alarm sounds in my head every time I need to send someone off. I haven't had to do it that often but, for some inexplicable reason, I've found that a red card often leads to the forming of some kind of bond between the referee and the dismissed player. The best example of this, in my particular case, occurred after I'd shown a red card for the first time.

I'd been refereeing in the Llanelli District for some three years when I had cause, during a game at Furnace, to dismiss one of the visiting Llandybie props, Duncan Price. It was a tension-filled match since Llandybie needed to win to ensure promotion, which they succeeded in doing. Having blown the final whistle I headed immediately for the changing room. At the Furnace ground the referee has to go through the players' changing facilities to get to his changing room, and I found Duncan had already started celebrating and was embracing a bottle of champagne. He called me over so that we might share the bottle and we spent some time socialising together. Following that incident we became friends and Duncan is now a referee himself.

Another problem for referees at the lower levels is that they can't always depend on support from assistant referees. Usually the assistants have connections with the participating teams and their allegiance to their particular clubs is greater than their desire to respect the laws of the game. I remember an incident at a second-team match at Pontyberem involving the Bont wing, Noel Bowen, who, on his day, was a really good player. But for the fact that the social side of rugby and enjoying a few beers was so important to him, he might well have gone on to play at a higher level. Noel received the ball out wide, ran over the touchline behind the linesman from the home club, Peter 'Jeanie' Griffiths, and grounded the ball in the corner! The poor referee was much too far behind the play to realise what had actually happened and he was given no indication by Mr Griffiths to suggest that anything untoward had occurred. The visiting Cydweli supporters were incensed and they berated the referee and his assistant for ages in the hope of convincing them that it was never a try. Noel's response was to tell them, 'Read the *Carmarthen Journal* next week, you'll find out whether it was a try!'

I don't think I've ever made such a bad decision but I've had cause to question the integrity of a few assistant referees. During my time in the lower divisions, one touch judge was so biased that I refused to allow him to continue after the first half. On the other hand, I have also disregarded the decisions of some unbiased assistants purely because I considered that I was in a better position to see than they were.

In fairness to assistant referees appointed by the union, or officially by the body responsible for a particular game or championship, they weren't allowed to step into the field of play to indicate an offence. They could only hold out their flag to stop play as a result of an incident, such as foul play, which the referee had been unable to see. But the assistant was not permitted to indicate a forward pass or an offside. They might say something to the referee, via the communication equipment that the officials wear, such as 'That pass was forward,' or 'Keep an eye on Number 7, he's breaking too early from the scrum,' but the referee was not obliged to listen. He would, on the other hand, be required to take their word with regard to offences such as a foot in touch or foul play.

Under the new laws introduced in 2008 the status of the official formerly called 'touch judge' was raised to 'assistant referee'. Now the assistant referee is allowed to draw the referee's attention to anything which he might not have seen. However, I must stress that the referee has the last word and he has the right, if he so chooses, to reject any advice which might be given by his assistant. This is why it is so important to have assistant referees whom you have total confidence and whom, more importantly, you can trust to make the right decision and not leave you exposed. I have been fortunate over the years that most of the touch judges assisting me have been very good and supportive, but in the last few seasons I have, unfortunately, had to inform Robert Yeman of one or two whom I do not want as assistants in any of my games again, due to their lack of support and incompetence whilst officiating at some very important matches.

It's customary for the authorities to ensure that there is always an experienced referee running the line when the match referee is comparatively inexperienced at a particular level, and I have benefited from that policy. I remember taking charge of a European Trophy match between Treviso and Connacht. I made a mistake during the first few minutes of not seeing a knock-on which resulted in a try being scored. It was only after awarding the try that I realised an offence had been committed. That affected my performance for the rest of the game, since the incident in question had shattered my confidence. One of the touch judges that day (along with Huw David, a great and honest colleague from Bridgend) was the experienced Dunvant referee, Robert G Davies. After the match he took me to one side and told me that he could see that my early mistake had been playing on my mind throughout the game, with the result that I hadn't been as focused as I should have been from that point onwards. He stressed that it was essential that I learned to forget about any such errors and that I carried on as if it hadn't happened because, after all, every referee is guilty of making mistakes. That was a timely and very valuable piece of advice which I have always tried to heed. Another piece of advice I can offer to young referees is that, having realised that they made a mistake they should never try and put it right by giving the opposition a decision purely to atone for the earlier error. Two wrongs never make a right.

Another useful aid for young referees in Wales, from which I personally derived great benefit, is the system whereby a number of refereeing coaches are appointed to look after a specific number of referees in the higher divisions of the union. They are non-salaried positions and the success of the scheme is down to the goodwill and co-operation of a number of former referees. I was fortunate in that I had one of the best as my coach, namely Derek Bevan, and he would come to watch me some six times a season. His role was completely different to that of the assessor, whose job was basically to point out where I'd gone wrong in a game. Derek would have a chat with me after a match and point out the positive aspects of my performance, whilst also noting some possible improvements. For example, he might suggest that I stand in a different position for certain phases depending on where they would occur on the field.

Derek continued with this work until 2007, during which time I learned a great deal from him; not only with regard to refereeing but also to the way I should conduct myself off the field. It's important that referees are respected both on and off the field. Ray Gravell was an excellent example of someone who paid homage to that particular belief for he would often pick up the phone to congratulate me after a good performance.

Since reaching the top as a referee I've also had to do my share of running the line in some big games. I naturally prefer refereeing, whilst fully realising that I'm also expected to officiate as an assistant referee from time to time. The guidelines for that particular duty are completely different, of course. Whilst the referee has to concentrate on play which occurs in the vicinity of the ball and endeavour to follow it around the field like some kind of flanker, the assistant referee's main duty is to watch what happens off the ball, often after play has moved on. Another discipline which the assistant must master, particularly if he's used to refereeing himself, is to refrain from telling the referee what he should do. In other words, he shouldn't try to carry out the referee's job for him. Whilst accepting that this can sometimes happen inadvertently it's a fact that some referees, when running the line, think they are better than the chap in the middle and that they should be refereeing the match, which can be the cause of considerable distress for the poor referee. But Robert Yemen tries to ensure that the officials he appoints for a particular game get on well with each other.

It was as a touch judge that I was introduced to top level rugby. I ran the line in a match between Pontypridd and Dunvant at Sardis Road in the old Welsh Heineken League competition for teams from Wales. I couldn't believe that I, a lad from the little village of Mynyddcerrig, was entering the Pontypridd changing room in order to check the studs of world-famous stars such as Neil Jenkins and Martyn Williams. But one of the disadvantages of being an assistant referee is that he is the closest official to both team benches and the supporters. As a result, he is the one who takes the most flak. This can be a daunting experience.

I remember some six years ago running the line in Cape Town in a match between South Africa and Australia. Two of the Australian coaching staff were following the game on the touch line. One was the defence coach (but was acting as a water carrier) and the other was a team doctor or physiotherapist. They whinged incessantly at nearly every decision that didn't go their way from the very beginning. They followed me up and down the touchline and shouted comments such as 'Oi, Touchie, watch the game, mate!' or 'Why don't you tell the ref what's going on out there!' or 'How come you didn't see that then, Touchie?' My patience eventually ran out and I turned to the water carrier and shouted at him in Welsh, 'Listen, if you don't shut your mouth I will shove that water bottle so far up your arse you will be seeing stars. Now piss off!' The amazed expression on his face was something to behold, and resulted partly from the fact that he had no idea in what language he had just been threatened. But they both got the message because I didn't hear a peep from them for the rest of the game. However, the water carrier might well know what I meant now, since he was John Muggleton and was appointed last season as the Scarlets defence coach! In fact, at a Heineken Cup meeting in Paris a few months ago, Garan Evans asked me what had I written in the Welsh version of this book (*Hanner Amser*) about John Muggleton, since some of the Scarlets players had apparently been discussing it the previous week. Well, if they haven't told him by now, I am sure he'll find out soon enough or maybe even read about it here in the coming months!

I confess that on one occasion I shamefully took advantage of the fact that the touch judge is an easier target than the referee for disgruntled supporters. I was refereeing in Pontypridd and at one point I blew for a forward pass by the home team. (When I looked on tape afterwards it was obvious that the pass wasn't forward, which was the opinion of the Ponty supporters at the time.) All hell broke loose so, in order to save face, I looked over at Colin Saunders, one of the tough judges who was also an experienced referee, and shouted, 'Thanks very much, Col,' and raised my thumb. The crowd now thought that it was Colin who had called the forward pass. This took a lot of pressure off me since he now became the butt of the crowd's threats and abusive comments for the rest of the game. He was very annoyed when we got to the changing room at half time but we're still friends.

Colin and I have had many great trips away, refereeing or officiating for one another, and I shall never forget when we went to the Under-19 World Cup tournament in Treviso in 2002. We were being driven around in brand new Alpha Romeo which, as part of the model's new design, didn't have normal handles to open the doors. They were part of the door itself and were located near the window, making them difficult to see – particularly for a boy from Mynyddcerrig who had never been near a car like that before. I was late, as always, so Colin and the driver were already in the car waiting for me. When I tried to open the back door I couldn't find the handle, so I shouted, 'Saunders, how do you get in these cars if there's no handle?' They were both laughing so much that they could not, or would not, get out to show me. They opened a window instead and made me climb in. The car had child-lock safety so I couldn't even put my hand through the open window and open the door from the inside. If anyone would have witnessed that incident they surely would have doubted whether I could be considered responsible enough to take charge of an important rugby match. I found the handles on the way back, though.

I've had a few memorable experiences off the field of play. I went to Belfast in November 2007 to referee in a Heineken Cup match between Ulster and Gloucester. The other match officials were Nigel Whitehouse (assistant referee), a police inspector based in Swansea; Barry Gregory (video referee), a chief inspector of police at Cardiff; and Jonathan Mason (assistant referee), who worked for the Crown Prosecution at the Swansea Law Courts. As usual we all went out for a meal together the night before the game. At about eleven o'clock we went back to the Hilton for a nightcap in the bar, which was quite empty and very quiet, before going to bed. Two big, tough-looking blokes with shaven heads were sitting at the bar and after a while three other chaps came in, and you could feel the tension of an argument brewing. After a few minutes they started fighting with each other. Nigel said, 'If this carries on, we are going to have to step in and stop it because we cannot, as police officers, be seen sitting here doing nothing.' 'Well,' I said, 'I ain't a police officer.'

It soon became a wild punch-up but when the biggest bloke, one of the shaven heads, began kicking one of the others as he lay on the ground, the 'representatives of law and order' in the bar decided that they should try and stop the fighting. Nigel and Barry waved their official warrant cards as they jumped into the fray, shouting, 'Stop! Stop! Police!' The shaven-headed one scanned the cards, which of course denoted that they both worked for police forces in South Wales, and dismissed them with the words, 'Those mean f*** all over here,' whereupon he started fighting again.

By this time I was hiding behind the piano and Jon Mason wasn't far behind me. It was a nasty situation and at one point one of the Irishmen threatened to bring a chair down on Nigel's head, so Mason and I thought we'd better go and help. Somehow we managed, with the assistance of a few others in the hotel bar, to persuade the fighters to stop and leave the hotel. In due course the police arrived and Nigel described to them what had happened. He was called aside a few minutes later and informed that the two shaven-headed ones had once been prominent members of the IRA and that there was a big family feud going on at one of Belfast's notoriously rough housing estates.

The following morning, the police got in touch with us to say that the previous night's fighting had continued on the local housing estate and that one of the shaven heads, having been badly stabbed, was now in intensive care in a critical but stable condition. Another man had been charged with attempted murder, so the police wanted the four of us to provide statements describing what had happened in the hotel bar. The last thing I needed before taking charge of a big match was to be stuck down the local nick for a few hours. The other three agreed to go but, because I like to have a few hours sleep during the afternoon before an evening game, I quickly retired to my bed and put the 'Do Not Disturb' sign up on the door, the hotel phone off the hook and my mobile on silent. I'm very glad that I did, for I heard afterwards that the police had told my fellow officials that they needn't be worried should they be required to return to Belfast for the court case, since they would be provided with adequate police protection during their visit!

That evening we returned to the hotel, got changed and decided to relax in the bar with a few beers, as we always do after a match. We thought it would be best not to venture out to experience the delights of the city that night; not because Ulster lost but in case we were marked men. We had only just settled down when the fire alarm went off and we all had to evacuate the hotel. 'That's it,' I said, whilst we were all drinking our beer outside in the cold, 'they have come to bomb us now because you have made statements!' Thankfully it was just some drunken young yob who had set the fire alarms off as a joke. I can assure you that only he found it funny that night. However, that was the only time I have had a bad experience in Belfast. I have found it to be a very welcoming city, and Ravenhill is one of my favourite club grounds as a referee.

Another incident comes to mind on the occasion of a game between Orrell and Toulon, in one of the first seasons of European rugby, which happened to be my first match as an official at that level. Derek Bevan and I were touch judges and Paul Adams the referee. We were staying in Wigan, which was only a few miles from the ground in Orrell, and after the match we headed back to the hotel to change before going out for the night. After a few beers in Billy Boston's pub, where we were given a great welcome as he is also Welsh, we moved onto a place that happened to be a karaoke pub. After a few pints I was in the mood for giving a song or two, the first of which was 'The Green Green Grass of Home'. It went down a treat. As a result I was forced back up to sing 'Delilah' and because they enjoyed it so much we didn't have to pay for any drinks for the rest of the evening.

We had a great night and on the way back to the hotel I decided that I wanted something to eat. The other two didn't feel hungry so they went on their way while I looked for somewhere where I might get a kebab. When I got back to the hotel the door to Paul's room was open, so I went in to see if he was all right. But he was already fast asleep and lying in his clothes on the bed. I was now starting to feel unwell and needed a toilet, so instead of creating a stink in my room I thought it would be more convenient to use Paul's bathroom. Just before leaving I was feeling very thirsty, thanks to a rather spicy kebab, so I drank a glass of water which I found in the bathroom. I downed it quickly before going back to my room. When I called by his room the following morning he was on all fours looking for something, which turned out to be his contact lenses.

'Where did you put them last night, then?' I asked. 'I don't remember,' he replied, 'but no matter how drunk I get I always take them out. Oh, God!' he continued. 'I remember now: I put them in a glass of water in the bathroom. I must have bloody swallowed them by mistake when I got up to go to the toilet last night and took a drink of water.' It was only on the way home that I realised it was me. I never mentioned it to him at the time but years later, during an address at a rugby function, I confessed that I was the one who had swallowed his contact lenses. (And before you make disparaging remarks about referees who can't see, I should add that Paul wore his glasses to referee his next match.) My next game was my best ever, for I was able to see what was going on from both ends, as it were! One player even remarked, 'Good God, Nigel, have you got eyes in your backside, man?' Little did he realise!

I remember my first overseas trip as a refereeing official mainly because I have never since experienced such generous hospitality. Huw Watkins, Derek Bevan and I went to the Italian city of Rovigo to officiate in the game between the home side and Bedford in the Heineken Cup. There was probably more than one reason why we had such a great welcome. It was the city where our fellow Welshman, the great Carwyn James, had spent some time coaching and he was still revered there. In addition, Derek was the best referee in the world at the time and our hosts were obviously mindful of that fact. However, the journey didn't get off to a particularly good start in my case. Apart from a school skiing holiday back in 1985 this was the only time I had travelled by air, so when we got to the check-in at Cardiff airport I was not entirely sure what I needed to do. For example, when I was given a luggage tag to fill in, I asked the others for the address of the hotel. Derek dictated, 'Number 1, High Street, Rovigo, SA1.' Only when I saw Huw on his knees, laughing, did I realise what they were up to.

As the rookie touch judge I had been given the job of carrying the metal case which housed the match flags and the electronic communication equipment that we would be using during the game. As I walked out of the airport terminal at Rhoose and across the tarmac towards our plane, Huw and Derek mischievously sent me in the wrong direction towards another aircraft located nearby. The case I was carrying looked very much like one which professional hit men might use to house a rifle and I probably looked very much like one of them as I made my way, on my own, across the runway. Then, in a flash, I was grabbed by two security men and taken to one side, as they considered my behaviour to be quite threatening. I managed to persuade them that I was harmless but not before I had been lectured on the dangers of careless behaviour at an airport. During all of this, Messrs Bevan and Watkins were tickled pink once again.

From the moment we arrived at Rovigo the club officials treated us like royalty. They sent a car to pick us up at the airport on the Friday night, which took us first to our hotel and then to an incredible feast at a local restaurant for the officials of both clubs and us. We were eating from 8.30 until past midnight – some sixteen courses in all – one of which I had never tasted previously or since, namely peacock, which I believe is illegal to eat in our country. Before we left for home we were taken to a very classy shop in order that we could take some gifts back for our families. I got a very nice bottle of whisky for my father, and the Rovigo officials insisted once again that they would pay for everything. In those days, taking part in such a prestigious tournament as the European competition was a new experience for a club like Rovigo, so they probably wanted to make an impression by treating the refereeing team and the various officials very well indeed. Yet I must say that when I returned there to officiate a few years later the hospitality was still very generous.

One of the pleasures of officiating away from home is having the opportunity to socialise with fellow members of the refereeing team. The usual routine on European or international weekends is to arrive in the city or country where we are refereeing at least a day before the match. Of course, if I am refereeing in the southern hemisphere then I will have arrived much sooner to acclimatise. In the evening, after all the formalities have been completed, we officials and a few others, such as the liaison officer and maybe the fourth and fifth official, will meet for dinner, either at the hotel or a nearby restaurant. I really enjoy this type of get-together on a Heineken Cup weekend, when we might be a team of Welsh officials working together. Although I won't drink the night before a match, apart from maybe a glass of wine or beer with the meal, we always have a great laugh and continually indulge in merciless leg-pulling. In fact the atmosphere is usually so relaxed that you would never think that we had such an important match the following day. During international or Heineken Cup final weekends the match officials are allowed to take partners along, which I have done on a few occasions. Everyone has been very welcoming and the fact that my partner is a man has made no difference at all.

The usual routine on match day is to have a walk around the town or city after breakfast and relax over a cup of coffee in the morning, or over a light lunch if we have an evening game. If there is time I like to have an hour or two's sleep before having a bath and getting ready to leave for the ground. If I am the referee, I will have a short meeting of about fifteen minutes with the two assistants, concerning what exactly I would like them to do during the match and in what way we can give the best performance possible as a team of officials working together. Every referee is different with regard to the way in which he wishes his assistants to perform their duties. One thing in particular I ask of my assistants, especially if the two teams concerned have a little history, is that they keep an eye on what takes place behind my back, or that they pay particular attention to what the two front rows get up to on my blind side of the scrum. I assure them that I will then take action if they draw my attention to any irregularities.

When I take charge of local matches I like to get to the field about an hour before kick-off. However, with regard to the big games I make sure that I arrive about an hour and a half before the match is due to start. Away from home I will relax in the hotel before leaving for the ground and, as I have mentioned, if it's an evening kick-off, I will have a nap during the afternoon. I will have something to eat for the last time some three hours before taking the field. That might be a late breakfast if it's an afternoon match or a late, light lunch if it's an evening kick-off. But wherever I stay and whatever time the game is due to start, my match-day meal is always a fried egg sandwich. This is something that began when I lived at home with my parents and has continued to this day.

My usual schedule in the stadium is to take a look at the pitch, take out the kit from my bag and then, usually in the company of my two assistants, have a word with both teams in their changing rooms. I often make a point of speaking with both front rows and remind them of the laws which apply to the scrum in particular, which are designed to ensure their safety and to prevent them from suffering any serious injury. I will remind them of the procedure before they pack down in the scrum, namely my giving the commands 'crouch, touch, pause, engage' with a pause between each, to which they must respond in turn. I emphasise the importance of effecting a forward shove as opposed to pushing upwards or downwards and stress that, should the whistle sound at any point, they must stop pushing at once. Referees are obliged to observe this drill in accordance with current guidelines. However, since I find myself refereeing some teams four or five times a season, I wouldn't need to go through all of that each time. I also have a word with both captains, but I generally find that the less I say before a game about my expectations as a referee the better it will be for all concerned. For, in the heat of the game, it would be quite easy for me to forget what I had said in the changing rooms. The last thing I need during a game is a know-all captain or a wise-guy player accusing me of going back on my word! Some referees like giving long speeches and address both teams at length. The well-liked Huw F Lewis falls into this category. I remember him emerging from a changing room after a ten-minute speech, complaining that the teams hadn't paid any attention. I told him that this was to be expected, since the two teams in question were the Wales Deaf Team and the New Zealand Deaf Team.

Huw is a lovely person who has made me laugh on many occasions. There is a story about him going to Ravenhill to referee an Under-21s match between Ireland and France about a week after the signing of the Good Friday Peace Agreement. Ian Paisley, who had of course been fiercely opposed to the agreement, happened to be having a meal at the hotel where Huw was staying. When a representative of the Irish Rugby Union called to take Huw to the stadium, he happened to notice Ian Paisley in the dining room. He offered to introduce Huw to the Rev. Paisley and, after the preliminary exchanges, there was a pregnant pause which was broken by Huw saying, 'You must be very pleased about the Good Friday deal and that you've reached agreement here in Northern Ireland.' Apparently Ian Paisley almost exploded and bellowed, 'Pleased? Pleased? The matter hasn't finished yet, not by a long way!' Huw retreated to Ravenhill having managed to disturb the peace and the status quo once again.

Before a game, coaches and players are permitted to speak with me regarding any issues or questions they may have.

After doing all the official stuff I normally switch my iPod player on. Sometimes I will plug into an iPod docking station system I take with me to the match or listen to it quietly as I get changed. Then it's out onto the field to do my pre-match warm-up routine which normally lasts no longer than about fifteen minutes. However, if it's cold and wet I quite often do it in the changing room! Normally I need to be back there about fifteen minutes before kick-off so that the communications guy can get us all wired up with the system we use to keep in touch with each other and with the link to the broadcaster.

Then it's 'forth into the lions' den'. I always try and get out into the tunnel before the players come out of their respective changing rooms. There is no particular reason for this, it's just a habit I suppose, but it's useful to see what tension there is as they walk out. It's also a good opportunity to make sure we hadn't missed any illegal clothing when we checked earlier, or to see if anyone has tried to be clever and not removed such items after we'd requested them to do so. To go out onto the field of play with any illegal clothing, such as padding or footwear, which they have been asked to remove earlier, is a red card offence, but I would rather deal with it before it gets that far.

Some coaches like to come up to me during half time in the hope of influencing me before the start of the second half, whilst others ask whether they should be saying anything in particular to their players during the break. Although I don't mind listening to complaints a coach might make, and sometimes I have to take their comments on board, I would never allow them to influence me in any way. Yet it's common practice for representatives of both teams to try and draw my attention to the ways in which their opponents are breaking the laws and are trying to deceive me as referee.

CHAPTER 8

To the Top

At the end of the 2001 season, the unique Derek Bevan retired from the WRU panel and from refereeing in general. After being the top referee in the world for many years and taking charge of forty-four internationals, he was finally calling it a day, meaning there was a vacancy within the top grade of refereeing in Wales. Each year, at the end of May, the advisors would meet to allocate all the referees to their grades for the coming season. A few weeks later we would receive a letter in the post from Clive Norling informing us of our position. It was with great delight that I learned that the referee taking Mr Bevan's place on the panel would be me.

My first game big game after being promoted to the panel grade was in October 2001 at St Helens, where Swansea were playing Caerphilly in the Welsh-Scottish League. It was also the first time I had refereed a match of that standard. I was a little nervous as I usually am when officiating for the first time at a particular level. So I was very glad on that occasion to have two good friends running the line: Nigel H Williams, who was a top-class international referee (and who continues to give me advice and encouragement), and Mark Sayers, an experienced referee from Llanelli. Perhaps the fact that Clive Norling, who managed the Welsh referees at that time, was there watching along with Robert Yemen, who was my assessor on the day, had made me more nervous than usual. It was an important day for a certain Gavin Henson as well, since he was making his debut for Swansea. The match report the following day in the *Western Mail* by George Williams, a genial man and a fine reporter, referred to the fact that a new star had appeared amongst Welsh rugby players. However, I took particular pleasure in reading his next sentence which mentioned that a new star had also emerged amongst Welsh referees.

The story could have turned out quite differently. During the game Matthew Robinson, the Swansea winger, caught a high kick behind his own line and called for a mark, as he was quite entitled to do. He then took a quick tap through the mark and grounded the ball in the in-goal area, following which he sprinted for the 22-metre line, took a hefty drop-kick upfield and raced in pursuit of the ball. None of the Caerphilly players were back to defend so there was no one there to stop Robinson from scoring a try had he been allowed to pick up the ball and dive over the Caerphilly line. But before he'd gone too far I blew my whistle and called him back. At the time I had no idea why I had done so, but I had an inclination that something was wrong. Scott Gibbs, the Swansea captain, and Robinson came up to me to ask why I had blown the whistle. Now, I couldn't confess that I didn't know so I hurriedly answered that I hadn't seen the Swansea winger actually kick the ball through the mark. Fortunately they accepted the explanation, took the mark free kick again and thankfully this time opted to kick for touch. After going home and consulting the law book, I was glad to discover that I'd made the right decision. It appears that the ball was dead once the mark was called and if he had restarted play by kicking through the mark and then grounded the ball whilst still behind his own line, then a five-metre scrum should have been awarded to Caerphilly. And that's what happened that day.

Since that incident I've had the feeling of 'what the hell happens now?' on more than one occasion. It usually occurs after a long hold up following an injury or a substitution. For a second or two I might find it difficult to remember, for example, why I blew for a scrum shortly before the break in play. I recall that happening once during an EDF Cup game between Gwent Dragons and Leicester Tigers at a wet and windy Rodney Parade. It was the first-ever match in this cross-border competition and the norm at the time was that Welsh referees would referee the matches in Wales and the English in England. That particular arrangement had no bearing at all on the way I approached or refereed the games, but it certainly did in the eyes of the supporters and sometimes the away team. That was the game which resulted in the start of my climb to the top of the refereeing ladder. After the match Derek Bevan, who was on the BBC commentary team, came into the changing room and said, 'Well, the boy has now become a man. That was a very good refereeing performance!'

However, halfway through the first half I didn't have a clue why I'd blown for a scrum a few minutes previously and Austin Healey, the Leicester scrum-half, had sensed that I had a problem. 'Whose ball, Ref?' he asked, thinking that he'd catch me out. 'Ours,' I said, pointing towards the Dragons, knowing that this would annoy him. In fact it annoyed him so much that he had a right go at me after Leicester lost. Now, many of you may ask yourselves if this story is true, as you may have heard it a few times before. Well, all I will tell you is that it must be, because Healey was a pundit for the BBC in the other EDF game that weekend and he described the incident in question as an example of the fact that 'the Welsh referee' was biased.

I was never keen on Healey's attitude on the field, for he talked incessantly and always tried to get one over on the referee in order to show that he was clever. If his side had lost and things hadn't gone his way, he was always ready to have a go at me. But if they had won then he was a different character altogether. But one must have respect for him as a player for he was very talented indeed. Other renowned 'talkers' were Lawrence Dallaglio and Agustín Pichot, but in general they were good blokes off the field and I had a lot of respect for them.

Another player I respect is John Hayes, the British Lions,

Ireland and Munster prop. As a member of the front row union he would often get penalised but, unlike some others of that fraternity, he would never complain, answer back or try and blame someone else, no matter how often it happened. I don't think he has received the praise he deserves as a player, particularly with regard to aspects of the game which tend to be disregarded by the critics. For example, in my opinion he is one of the best line-out lifters of the modern era, which is such an important aspect of rugby today.

Lawrence Dallaglio had a certain presence on the rugby field and, like John Smit, Richie McCaw, Ryan Jones and Martin Johnson, he was an excellent leader. He always liked to bring his influence to bear on the referee, particularly an inexperienced one, but it was possible to get to know how he operated. After being penalised, he would always appear very remorseful and try to give the impression that he'd not had any intention of transgressing. I recall being duped by him in a game between Wasps and Toulouse in the Heineken Cup. The French had been pressurising the Wasps' line for quite some time when Dallaglio went in from the side and killed the ball. I blew at once and awarded a penalty to Toulouse, whereupon Dallaglio immediately apologised, 'Sorry, Ref, I thought the ball was out!' That split-second distraction was enough to prevent him from getting a yellow card, although he deserved one, and I could tell from his expression a second later that he knew full well that the ball wasn't out. That served as an important lesson for me. Since then, I have always worked on the principle that players are usually fully aware of what they're doing when they break the rules. I had cause to show Dallaglio a yellow card on a few occasions after that, so he got away with it in Toulouse for the first and last time. Whenever I refereed him in later years he knew who was in charge.

I have already referred to the fact that the games I refereed professionally were much faster and that consequently I needed to be much fitter. With this in mind, and in accordance with the criteria laid down by the IRB for the appointment of international referees, I have to undergo fitness tests four times a year. The testing is usually done at the WRU's Elite Training Centre at Hensol in the Vale of Glamorgan, where Huw Wiltshire measures my performance with three kinds of running tasks: the dreaded bleep test, which I despise yet have to pass at a specific level; a sprint test covering 10, 20, 30, and 40 metres; and finally a Phosphate Decrement Test over 30 metres. These are all designed to ensure that my speed and recovery powers are up to standard. I pass the test every time but I must confess that I'm not as fit as when I turned professional some eight years ago. My age is catching up on me. Going professional also meant that I had to be more alert. The pace of the game is quicker so the referee has less time to think before making a decision. I was required not only to see what was going on in front of me but also to predict what was *likely* to happen, so that I could be in the right place at the right time. I hope I still have that ability.

I have been very fortunate in that, since becoming a professional referee, I have only had to miss one or two games because of injury. Yet I learned years ago that it's always better to choose not to officiate rather than do so without being fully fit. I remember refereeing in Connacht after having had trouble with my back for a few days. This is an occupational hazard for referees who spend so much time driving, flying, sitting in airport lounges and sleeping in strange and often uncomfortable beds. During that particular game my back condition deteriorated badly with the result that I was having difficulty keeping up with play. As was to be expected, this had a detrimental effect on my overall performance and I got poor marks from my assessor for that match. After that I decided never to take the field in the future unless I was fully fit, since to do otherwise would be an injustice to myself and, more importantly, to the players and the match in question.

Injuries to players during a game can be a nightmare,

particularly for a referee who is not very alert. Although he might not be at fault in any way, a nasty accident can play on the mind of a referee since he naturally asks himself afterwards whether he could have done anything to prevent it from happening. The referee must react quickly when a bad injury occurs; first by blowing his whistle to stop play immediately and to prevent any further injury. He then must make sure that the medical people on the sidelines are made aware of the situation and that they come on straight away to attend to the injured player. Quite often the reaction of the other players is a good indicator of how serious an injury might be. At other times it's obviously so serious that the referee has no reason to hesitate – as in the case of the injury suffered by Robin Sowden-Taylor, the Wales and Blues flanker, in 2006. During a match against the Ospreys which was televised live on S4C, I heard the crack as his ankle bone broke and I could see at once that his foot was facing the wrong way – that is, it was pointing backwards. The programme producers fortunately saw fit not to show a replay of the incident. That was one of the worst injuries I have witnessed in any game I have refereed.

Yet the game in which I was given my biggest fright happened years ago when I was refereeing many schoolboy district matches, such as the Dewar Shield competition for schoolboys under 15. (I enjoy looking back over old match programmes from that period and noting the youngsters who went on to play first class rugby and, more interestingly perhaps, who amongst them disappeared off the rugby scene.) One day I was refereeing a match in that competition between Mynydd Mawr and the visiting north Wales team. After a scrum I noticed that one of the visitor's props, a farmer's son from Machynlleth, was lying lifeless on the ground. I really thought that he'd broken his neck, so I stopped the game immediately and before long an ambulance arrived to take him to hospital. I was really shaken to see a young lad in such a helpless state on the field. I wrote to him some time afterwards to ask how he was getting on. He thanked me for taking the trouble to enquire about him and told me that the injury wasn't as bad as people first feared and that he was hoping to be back playing again soon. It was great to learn that he felt well enough to think about returning to the game.

Younger players gave me my first taste of refereeing at international level. At around the same time as turning professional, I was invited to referee, along with Colin Saunders from Wales, at the Under-19 World Cup which was being held in northern Italy. My big match in the tournament was between South Africa and New Zealand in the semi-final at Treviso. It was an open game with the All Blacks winning 42-20, partly as a result of a great display by their outside half, a lad called Luke McAllister, who has caused problems for many teams at the highest level since then. I thought I handled the game rather well and I obtained high marks from the assessor, Gabriel Villari from Italy. That was possibly why I was invited the following year to officiate at the Under-21 World Cup Competition in Johannesburg instead of Huw Watkins, who had injured his calf in a play-off match at Aberavon, at which point I had to take his place. I took charge of the semi-final, which was once again between South Africa and New Zealand. It was one of the hardest and most exciting games that I have ever refereed. It was played in a university stadium in front of a huge crowd who seemed to enjoy it immensely. South Africa won by 19-17 and the press praised not only the standard of the rugby but also of the referee, which was rather nice to read. It might well have been a different story had South Africa lost, for I don't think there is any rugby-playing country in the world that likes winning as much as South Africa.

That was my first visit to South Africa, and spending three weeks there was a memorable experience which placed me on the first rung of the international ladder. Despite the pleasures of visiting the attractions of that delightful country, such as Sun City and the wildlife of the Kruger National Park, I shall never forget the sight of the shanty towns and young children begging at the side of the road for food, clothes or money as we travelled from the airport to our hotel in Johannesburg. The country has made huge strides since the abolition of apartheid, but there's no doubt that there's a lot of work still to be done in order to raise the standard of living of those poor people.

I returned to South Africa a few months later to run the line in a Tri Nations match. During a previous Tri Nations game, a stupid supporter had run on to the field and attacked the referee David McHugh. As a result, security had been stepped up. We weren't allowed to go anywhere, not even just outside the hotel, without having huge minders to protect us. One morning I went to the gym and, as expected, I had the company of a security guard. He also got changed into keep-fit gear, but what startled me was hearing a loud 'clunk' from his coat when he threw it down on a bench. He had a large gun in his pocket! I remember feeling rather downhearted at that point as I realised how much the refereeing world had changed. However, I'm glad to say that the country now appears to have greater stability and that there's no longer a need for guns to protect referees and their assistants.

The electronic equipment which forms part of the modern age of professional refereeing took some getting used to. At first, hearing the comments and directions of touch judges through a little implement in my ear was a strange experience, as they themselves had to get used to talking to the referee through a little device on their flag stick. The system wasn't perfect and occasionally failed to work. I remember that happening up in Pontypool in a game against Bedwas. As a result I asked the two touch judges to revert to the old system of communicating with their hands when they wanted to attract my attention, but to do so inconspicuously and without any fuss. Just before half time, Bedwas crossed the home team's line following a final pass which was rather flat but which, in my opinion, wasn't forward, so I awarded a try. Meanwhile Phil Fear, one of the touch judges, was still standing on the Pontypool 22 metre line and making vigorous signs with his arms that the pass was forward. But I didn't think it was, so I took no notice of him and played on. The home supporters, however, had seen Phil's gesticulations and they were up in arms that I had chosen to disregard him. When I walked off at half time they were baying for my blood!

By now the technology has improved a lot and the communications system, consisting of microphones which link the referee, his assistants and the video referee, is quite sophisticated. However, when a game is being televised the referee has to wear an additional microphone which enables everyone at home to listen to what he's saying. That can be quite dangerous, particularly if the referee in question is, like myself, prone to coming out with a few swear words from time to time.

The first time I refereed a game which was being televised live, Pontypridd were playing Glasgow at Sardis Road in an evening match which was being shown on S4C. The weather during the day was so bad that I had a telephone call asking me to take a look at the pitch at two o'clock. At that time, although there was a little surface water, conditions were good enough to allow the game to proceed. But to play safe I arranged to undertake another inspection at five o'clock, one hour before the scheduled kick-off. No referee likes to cancel games because of adverse weather conditions but the players' safety is the most important consideration, and if there are any doubts on that score then cancellation is the only option. Indeed, if the referee deems a pitch to be playable but the teams are unwilling to take the field, he would have to respect their wishes. But he would remind them that his report to the union would have to note that, in his opinion, the match should have been played.

In this particular instance, the Glasgow team had already arrived by five o'clock and the television producer was like a cat on a hot tin roof, fearful that there would be no game to televise. Now, although such factors are not supposed to influence a referee's decision, they certainly added to the weight on my comparatively inexperienced shoulders. When I went out to inspect the pitch the rain had stopped, although conditions were very heavy underfoot. I believed the ground was firm enough to allow the game to proceed. Providing there was no more heavy rain we would be able to complete the full eighty minutes so that the result could stand. After consulting both team captains and coaches and ensuring that they were happy to give it a go, I confirmed that the game was on. In fact the playing surface was fine for the first half, but during the interval there was a very fierce hailstorm and an exceptionally strong wind began to blow. It was so powerful that it literally raised the roof of the stand a good couple of inches. Cenydd Thomas, an ex-international referee who was on the board at Pontypridd and who always looks after the referees well at Sardis Road, came into the changing room at half time. He expressed his grave concern that it was now unsafe not only for the players but also for the spectators sitting in the stand. I went out on to the field before the start of the second half and all I could see was a huge lake. It would have been impossible to continue so that was the end of my first game as a television referee.

Following bad weather, the matter of having to decide whether a pitch is playable or not can sometimes be a huge responsibility for a referee. I remember such an incident at Stradey Park on Boxing Day 2005, when I was due to referee the Scarlets against the Ospreys for the first time. I was really looking forward to taking charge of what was Wales' – if not one of Europe's – biggest derby match. There had been a severe frost and, although the Stradey staff had tried to cover the playing surface, parts of it, particularly in front of the stand, were still like granite when I got there about an hour and a half before the scheduled start. Gareth Jenkins, the Scarlets coach, was of the opinion that the pitch was playable and, as the ground staff were working hard on it, there was no point in rushing to make a decision. In any event, most of those intending to be at Stradey that afternoon had already arrived or would have started on their journeys. I tended to agree with him and thought that waiting until nearer kick-off would allow more time to get rid of the problem. Simon Easterby, the Scarlets captain, had already indicated that he was keen to play, so it was now a matter of waiting for the arrival of Duncan Jones, his Ospreys counterpart, in order to obtain his opinion. However, when Lyn Jones, the Ospreys coach, saw the condition of the pitch, he was not so keen to play. But he agreed that it would be just as well to wait a little longer for the ground staff to finish working on it, since Stradey Park was by now full to capacity. After warming up on the pitch, Duncan Jones stated that he wasn't happy to play and both he and Lyn wanted to postpone the game. By that time the kick-off was only twenty minutes away, but since one of the teams was unwilling for the match to go ahead I had no choice but to call it off. Standing in front of an angry holiday crowd of 12,000 and representatives of the media and the press to confirm that the match would not take place is not a duty I would want to undertake again in a hurry!

In taking such a decision, a referee must give priority to the well-being of the players and if Duncan Jones and his team were of the opinion that their safety would be jeopardised if the game went ahead then their wishes had to be respected. It didn't matter that there were television cameras present or that there was a raucous crowd of thousands anxious for the game to be played. I was harshly judged for days afterwards. However, those who complained didn't realise that it hadn't been my decision alone but that I'd had to call it off not only due to safety considerations but because the Ospreys team didn't believe that the state of the pitch was good enough. I've got to say, though, that postponing the game was the correct decision on the day.

Some three weeks before the storm-affected game at Pontypridd, I'd agreed to take part in a concert in aid of cancer research at Pontyberem. It had been arranged by the singer Gwenda Owen, who had herself been cured of cancer. I was then informed that I was required to take charge of Pontypridd v Glasgow on the same evening as the concert, so I had to apologise for not being able to take part after all. However, since the match had finished early, I was able to shoot back to Pontyberem and appear on stage. I got quite a few laughs when I told the audience that I'd made a special effort to be there by calling off an important rugby match at half time.

I never need much persuasion to make tracks for Pontyberem. That's where I live and I really enjoy socialising at the local rugby club where, on a Saturday night in particular, I take great pleasure from being in the company of old friends. I used to train regularly with the village rugby team but that became too much of a strain on this body of mine, although I still join their sessions when I make a special effort to get fit during the summer months. I also feel very proud that the club has seen fit to put up a display case to house a few of the jerseys I have worn when refereeing some important matches.

Yet trying to keep a balance between my refereeing duties and being enticed back to Pontyberem can be difficult and even costly at times. The introduction of games on Friday evenings has been a blessing in my case since they allow me sometimes to go and see Pontyberem play on Saturday afternoons. On one occasion I was refereeing in Ireland on a Friday night and was keen to get back to the village by the following afternoon to watch the local derby against Tumble. I could only get a flight to Birmingham and it would be touch and go whether I made it on time. I put my foot down hard but, on the Heads of the Valleys road on the way down towards Glynneath, I came towards one of those dreaded speed camera vehicles which was parked in a lay-by. By the time I saw it, it was too late. I wasn't certain how fast I was going before I put the brakes on, but I was pretty sure it was more than the national speed limit. When the ticket came in the post a few weeks later it said I had been doing 97 mph. I couldn't believe I was going so fast so I decided to question the reading, with the result that my case had to be heard in court. Because I wanted the proceedings to be conducted in Welsh, almost a year went by before I appeared before the bench. I was quite worried as to the possible outcome, since at the time I was already carrying six penalty points on my licence and a further six would be enough to keep me off the road for a while. Fortunately, the magistrates issued only five penalty points and imposed a fine of £120 – all because I was in a hurry to get back home to watch Pontyberem play Tumble!

Having been chosen to be on the IRB touch judging panel I had to familiarise myself with a new task, namely acting as a video referee in some matches. Some hate that particular duty, for example Chris White, who gets very nervous when he has to do it. I have to say that it doesn't bother me as such but there's a much greater buzz to be had from being on the field itself. The video ref is usually put in a little cubby hole at the top of the stand or in one of the vans of the television company responsible for filming the game. Sometimes in club matches in France, you are sitting in the changing room with a little monitor in front of you. Thankfully I haven't had that experience but a few of the guys who have acted as video referees for some of the matches I have refereed out there have had to endure that discomfort, and sometimes come out of the changing rooms to the side of the pitch to pass their verdict on a try when the system isn't working properly. The video ref can either be completely on his own or have other officials or television staff sharing the room with him. I must confess that it was as a video referee that I had my greatest panic ever whilst part of a refereeing team. At Cape Town 2005 during a game between South Africa and the All Blacks, I was sitting in a room in the stand with the referee's assessor,

Giovanni Rommani from Italy and an official from the South African rugby union who was gathering statistics for him, and a technician who was responsible for ensuring that the picture on my TV and the sound connection linking me to the referee, Andy Cole of Australia, were in order.

I was watching the game through a window in front of me but from where I was sitting it wasn't possible to get a clear view of all the field, especially the nearest corner in the South African half. As a result, each time play reached that spot I had to stand up in order to see what was happening. That was the case when Daniel Carter kicked for the corner and the ball was taken over the touchline by the Springboks defence, leaving New Zealand to throw in five metres from the goal line. I thought to myself: this is it, now; the All Blacks are going to win the line-out then drive over and Andy Cole is going to ask me whether the ball was grounded properly for a try. I sat down quickly so that I could concentrate on the television pictures, but when I looked the screen was in complete darkness. I think my heart must have stopped for a second before I shouted at the technician to try and sort the problem out. Think about it: the referee asks me if it was a try and I have to say, 'Sorry, Andy, I don't know because I haven't got a picture!' The technician gave the set a few slaps but still no picture. Down he went on his knees, pulling out a few cables and stuffing a few others into different sockets, but nothing worked; I was still without a picture.

Fortunately by this time South Africa had relieved the pressure on their line and kicked the ball upfield. But there might have been a demand for a contribution from me at any moment so it was important to try and get the TV to work at once. As the poor technician was telephoning the programme director to tell him what had happened, Giovanni reached for a switch at the bottom of the TV and pressed it. The picture reappeared, much to everyone's relief. As I had leaned forward to try and see the play through the window, I had struck the switch and inadvertently turned the TV off. I called to the technician that we no longer had a problem since the picture had returned of its own accord, and I left it at that!

Some people are critical of the fact that referees are too ready to turn to the video referee for assistance. For my part, if I can see that a try has been scored I won't ask for the assistance of the television screen, but some referees like to get the video ref to confirm what they *think* they saw. I have to say that at times, having played back an incident on the screen, I have been surprised to find the evidence indicates that what I *thought* I had seen was completely wrong. I was running the line once in a match between Ireland and Italy at Lansdowne Road when Tommy Bowe scored what I and the referee, Dave Pearson, considered to be a perfectly good try. However, when I stood behind the posts for the conversion I could see, on the action replay on the ground's big screen, that the winger had dropped the ball as he endeavoured to ground it. The noise made by the crowd as they witnessed the incident again seemed to confirm that. Now, if Dave had asked for the video referee's assistance before awarding the try, people would have thought he was losing it! It was too late by that time to do anything about it. So, since that experience, I will only award a try if I am 110% sure it has been scored. If I have the slightest doubt at all I will pass the decision on to the video referee. After all, the most important thing for us all is that we get the decision right.

It is also important to ask the right question. I remember refereeing an EDF semi-final at the Millennium Stadium between Leicester and Wasps. Leicester set up a maul and drove over the Wasps line. I thought they had grounded the ball but I considered it wise to make sure, so I asked the video ref, Derek Bevan, 'Derek, I'm happy with the grounding of the ball; is there any reason why I can't award the try?' Much to my amazement, and that of everyone who was listening, Derek coughed (an indication perhaps that something was wrong) and answered, 'Nigel, you can't award the try because the ball was not grounded!' So now I tend to ask, 'Is it a try, yes or no?' We took some stick in the press over that incident but at the end of the day the important thing was that we had come to the right decision.

At present, a referee has the right to ask for video assistance when a player undertakes to ground the ball in the in-goal area (i.e. over the try line) or is in the act of grounding the ball. This basically means that if a player's foot is on the touchline and his next step is to score a try, then you can ask for assistance. If he put his foot on the touchline a few steps further out, you cannot consult the video ref.

Here's another example of the constraints to which referees are subjected. If a player knocks the ball on as he is about to score or, let's say, is within a metre of scoring, then you can 'go upstairs' as it were. If he knocks the ball on a couple of metres out, then, again, you cannot go to the video ref and will have to live by your own decision. It is evidently a grey area and an aspect of the game that always causes much debate between officials and the authorities when trying to determine the best possible protocol with regard to video referees.

Some would like to see this facility extended to allow calling for the assistance of the video referee within, say, five metres of the try line or for different offences in various areas of the pitch. In my opinion the ruling is fine as it is; otherwise it would be difficult to know where to draw the line. The only change that I would recommend would be to allow video evidence with regard to serious foul play which the referee may have missed on the field of play.

CHAPTER 9

Jonathan and the Media

THE WELSH TELEVISION PROGRAMME *Jonathan* was responsible for giving me quite a prominent profile away from the rugby field. At first I was recognised more often as one of the show's presenters than as a rugby referee. The idea originated in New Zealand where a very popular rugby-orientated programme would be shown the night before some important All Blacks games. The most important ingredient in the Welsh version was humour, and with that in mind Jonathan himself suggested my name to Matthew Tune, the producer, and Emyr Afan of Avanti Television. Based on my track record on stage and on other TV programmes, it was thought that I could inject a little comedy and, in the light of my refereeing experience, introduce an element of order and discipline to the proceedings. Jonathan was also a familiar figure, following his time with Neath Rugby Club, and was aided by the humorous input of the former Neath and Wales player Rowland Phillips, who also became part of the team. I have to admit that before joining the show I had no idea that Rowland was such a larger than life character. Eleri Siôn, a sports presenter who brought glamour and certain vitality to the show, completed the line-up.

From the beginning all four presenters got on very well with each other and that was the main reason why we had such a laugh putting the programme together, although at times we certainly pushed each others' patience to the limit. The two main script writers were the brothers Daniel and Matthew Glyn. It was rather ironic that they were so successful since, particularly during the early days, they didn't have a clue about rugby or sport in general. I remember at one point Gareth Edwards being suggested as a possible guest for the programme, only for Matthew to admit that he had no idea who he was. We had the same response a couple of years later with regard to Shane Williams.

We would usually meet on a Monday to read through the script in order to make any changes that were required before the programme was recorded the following night. Although the script gave an essential framework to the show, we were always free to ad-lib as we thought fit at the time. Sometimes these comments were quite *risqué* but the programme went out well after the nine o'clock watershed. Complaints were very few and the presenters rarely had cause to protest that the material was too blue.

Yet there were one or two items which I considered to be a little over the top and best omitted. I recall a suggestion that I should wear leathers for one sketch, to which I objected. After all, I was by that time required to referee at a fairly high level and it would be difficult for players to take me seriously on the field of a Saturday after being seen acting the clown on television the night before. But there were quite a few players who enjoyed watching the programme, many of whom were not Welsh speaking, in Wales and beyond.

During its run over a number of years, tens of thousands of viewers, many of whom lived outside Wales, tuned in and made *Jonathan* one of the most popular programmes on S4C. In the end we had rather a cult following.

Once I'd 'come out' (after the first series of *Jonathan*), I left myself open to all kinds of cracks about the fact that I was gay. For the next few years I was a constant target for my fellow presenters, but their teasing didn't worry me at all and when it occurred I was usually quite happy to join in the fun. My only cause for concern was that, in due course, the viewers would think the subject had run its course. If there had been another series, I think we would have had to agree to stop milking the fact that one of us was gay.

The first reference to my being gay was made in a New Year's Eve 'special'. I had 'come out' during the previous summer and, although the media had not made reference to this, it was fairly common knowledge. So the script writers decided in their wisdom that it would be funny if I 'came out officially', as it were, on TV. I agreed to run with this idea but I didn't want to make it a big issue. I preferred to treat the subject with a little subtlety so that the viewers and the studio audience, without being told categorically that I was gay, would have to decide for themselves whether that was the case in the light of what was said on the show. The show opened in my absence, with the other presenters asking, 'Where's Nigel, then?' Eleri then said, 'It's odd that he's not here because he said he was coming out tonight!' With that, a closet door opened on the set and I stepped out to the sound of the song 'I Am What I Am'. Nothing was actually said about my being gay and we got on with recording the rest of the show. Of course, in nearly all the shows after that there were 'gay' references and jokes in the script, and even if there weren't the cast would certainly ad-lib some. Yet it was surprising how many viewers thought for many years afterwards that the business of making cracks about my being gay was one big joke.

That programme had been recorded a few nights before New Year's Eve and my problem was finding a way of keeping all those provocative comments about my 'coming out' from my parents. After all, they'd only just come to terms with the shock of hearing that I was gay. I wanted to try and protect them from being hurt again when they watched the show and realised that I was now proclaiming the fact to one and all, so I formulated a plan. For many years my parents and I, along with practically everyone else in the village, would go to the Mynyddcerrig Social Club on New Year's Eve. Indeed, ever since the millennium celebrations I'd been doing a spot there as a comedian and singer on that night, with the exception of the year in question and the previous year. Because I had to referee on New Year's Day on those two occasions I decided to spend the night at home in Pontyberem. But since my parents did not like to miss *Jonathan* they'd programme the video recorder to record that night's show. So while they were at the club, I went to their house and pulled out the video recorder plug. However, because there was no live music in the club that night, a number of members went into the television lounge to watch *Jonathan*, including my parents. So they saw the whole programme after all but they never once spoke of it afterwards. In fact I am pretty sure that my father didn't understand the closet reference and he certainly wouldn't have realised the significance of the song lyrics. While I was at home that night I received a number of text messages from various cousins and friends saying that the references to my 'coming out' were very amusing, so that was of some consolation to me.

One reason for the series' success was the contribution of the audience. Some would come regularly to the recording sessions and there was never a shortage of clubs and societies that wished to participate in the fun. But I remember one young lady who had too much fun in the bar before we started to record. She was sitting in the front row and suddenly threw up all over my shoes and trousers. She was taken away but the incident left the production team with all kinds of continuity problems. However, that wasn't the first time that my 'wardrobe' was soiled during filming. On one programme we had weather presenter Sian Lloyd as a guest, and I had to present a forecast. When I referred to rain, Rowland threw a bucket of water over me. When I predicted a strong wind, a huge fan on the set blew a deluge of water over me. I ended the piece by saying, 'Next week, the weather is going to be rather shitty.' You can imagine, I'm sure, what happened next. Well, not quite, but my head and my clothes were covered in liquid chocolate!

One of the items I enjoyed filming most, and which

apparently also gave viewers at home a lot of pleasure, was when Rowland and I went to a farm in West Wales to catch some piglets in order to race them. It was hard work at times but we had a lot of fun, despite landing in a few filthy puddles. However, it wouldn't have been funny if the sow had got to us. She went wild and tried to get out of her pen as she heard her litter squealing, as they are prone to do. But I'm glad to say that the piglets were not harmed in any way and neither were the two presenters.

There were also experiences to forget, for example being rolled down a hill inside a giant ball. I was never a big fan of fairground rides when I was a kid, let alone being strapped inside a massive ball and sent hurtling down the hill. After filming that morning I went straight to bed and felt quite ill all day. That's the most unpleasant thing I've ever done, apart from eating a dog-food sandwich with the crazy *Dirty Sanchez* gang. However, that was better than some of the tasks which Jonathan and Rowland had to undertake. For example Rowland, on one occasion, had to eat a large spoonful of the hottest chilli they could find. But I think one of Jonathan's experiences was worse. He had an elastic band put around his forehead which was then pulled back and released. He was in agony, poor chap, and was left with a cut across his forehead.

When the *Jonathan* series ended last year, I think we were ready to admit that it had run its course or that it at least needed to be rested for a while. For my part, refereeing at the highest level means I'm subjected to more pressure and have to travel far more. I also have to undertake extra training to ensure that I maintain the required standard of fitness. Therefore, committing myself regularly to a programme like *Jonathan* would be difficult at present. Yet I suspect that when the programme was discontinued many viewers missed the buzz which it created during the international season. I used to be surprised that it drew such a positive response from people. However, that which gave me cause for concern was hearing children of eight or nine saying how much they enjoyed watching it, for it was, of course, directed at an adult audience and was shown late at night so that young children would not be able to see it. Yet I knew of one ten-year-old lad from Pontyberem who would go to stay with his grandmother every Friday night when *Jonathan* was televised so he could watch it, because his father wouldn't allow him to do so at home since he considered him to be too young. It appears that he wasn't the only one.

I certainly became a familiar face as a result of the programme but not everyone recognised me. I remember going on a blind date with a chap in Cardiff a few years ago. He obviously thought that he'd seen me somewhere before, but I didn't give him my real name just in case we didn't get on. The following day he happened to tell a mutual acquaintance, 'You'll never guess who I had a date with last night! It was Jonathan Davies!' When I told Jonathan the story he wasn't too pleased! In fact others have commented on the fact that we look alike, some even thinking that we're brothers. Apparently Sean Fitzpatrick, the former All Black hooker who regularly appears as a pundit on Sky, would send Jonathan a text message before a game which I was due to referee, saying, 'Your brother's refereeing again today!'

It's surprising how many people approach me when I'm out enjoying myself. It can be a nuisance at times, but generally having people tell me how much they appreciate what I do is very pleasing. Some ask for an autograph while others, particularly young girls, want to have a photograph taken with me. It annoys the Pontyberem boys that I, the gay member of the group, am able to 'pull' the smart girls. But the fact that I'm well known outside the village doesn't impress my mates at all. They always make sure that my feet remain firmly on the ground and if I don't have a particularly good game as a referee, they will be the first to tell me. They will also make sure that no one gives me any hassle when we're all out together –

Relaxing with the wives of some of the World Cup refs and officials.

With Dan and Rob Hayward at the Victoria and Albert Museum, London, when I was awarded the Stonewall Sports Personality of the Year.

A dinner for the officials and their partners in the hotel whose hospitality was so good during World Cup week. A night to remember. Everybody sang and had a great time.

Tara and Mali, who are very faithful and great company.

My first cap, with Hugh Watkins and Nigel Whitehouse, my linesman, out in Japan, 2005.

One of the first foreign trips, refereeing Llanelli on their first tour of Hungary at the end of the summer. With the band Jac y Do, who were performing there at the time – an unforgettable trip with these characters!

Modelling at a charity fundraiser at the Cardiff Hilton. I don't think I was destined for the catwalk, but I'll do anything for a good cause.

Me and Tony Spreadbury at the World Cup. Spreaders was one of those unique characters, always ready to lend a hand.

Proud smiles all round at Caersalem chapel during my godchild Ffion Haf's christening.

Sightseeing in Paris with Chris White's family – Lynn and the kids, Rhiannon, Deri and Sian.

The changing room in Argentina before the Argentina v Samoa match. This was the game and the performance that got me back climbing the international ladder. The worst changing room ever, a portakabin under the stand.

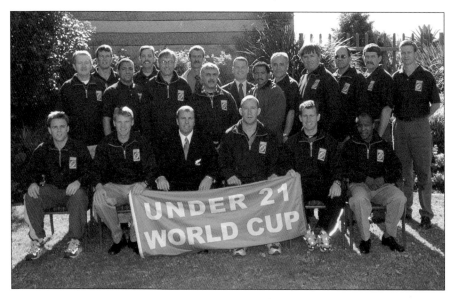

Under 21 World Cup officials in South Africa. An unforgettable time in an unique country.

Me and the guitar – which I can't play – in a fundraising concert for Air Ambulance Wales.

Giving the audience the red card for whistling at the ref on Jonathan Davies's programme!

Modelling the new Underarmour kit with Ryan Jones, Welsh Captain, 2008.

(Photo: Huw Evans Agency)

With the boss, Robert Yeman: me, Tim Hayes, Hugh Watkins, and James Jones.
(Photo: Huw Evans Agency)

Me and Simon McDowell. We're both celebrating our birthdays on the same day, in South Africa at the Under 21 World Cup. I've only been home for my birthday once in the last eight years.

Forced to put English captain Steve Borthwick in his place in the test match in Auckland, summer 2008 – a very difficult game to referee.

Gay whistle-blower quick with a quip

Welsh referee an original who moonlights as a stand-up comedian and singer

BY STUART DYE

THE man in the middle faces his toughest test at Eden Park tonight as he enters the cauldron of an All Blacks vs Wallabies match.

Welshman Nigel Owens is relatively inexperienced, having held the whistle for only five internationals, including Japan against Ireland and England versus Italy in the Six Nations.

But those matches are unlikely to compare with the atmosphere of tonight's crucial Bledisloe Cup and Tri-Nations decider.

The 35-year-old declined an interview as he was unable to clear it with his International Rugby Board bosses yesterday. "I don't want it to be my first and last [Tri-Nations]," he said.

But there is every chance his col-

ourful and unconventional background will stand him in good stead for a match sure to be awash with controversy.

In his spare time, Owens — a professional referee for five years — is a stand-up comedian and singer. He is a regular on television in Wales too. He is also the game's only openly gay professional referee.

Owens told a Welsh newspaper earlier this year he had contemplated suicide while struggling with his sexuality.

But the support of his family — and his sense of humour — got him through. "I might get someone shout something about me being a 'bent ref' but they usually realise what they've said and go 'Oh sorry Nige, didn't mean it like that'," he said.

He also spoke of the difficulty of being homosexual in a sport with such macho traditions. "It's such a big taboo to be gay in my line of work I

> **This is what it's all about, I'm going to enjoy every moment.**
> NIGEL OWENS

had to think hard about it [coming out] because I didn't want to jeopardise my career."

It seems that decision has done nothing to hinder his career with Owens selected as the only Welsh referee for the World Cup in France in

September.

But before that he faces his biggest challenge so far in his refereeing life tonight. In an interview with Super14.com, he said he was relishing the thought. "There will be pressure to perform and I'll be thinking during the anthems 'This is what it's all about, I'm going to enjoy every moment'."

The experience in stand-up comedy could come in useful in a fixture where tempers are bound to flare up. Refereeing at the Hong Kong Sevens in 2005, Owens told an argumentative Argentinian player: "You have two ears and one mouth — use them in proportion."

And if the occasion threatens to overwhelm him tonight, the Herald has some advice — watch for Aussie backs offside.

HUMOUR: Nigel Owens knows how to laugh.
PICTURE / GETTY IMAGES

A headline from the back page of one of New Zealand's daily rags, the morning before the big match between New Zealand and Australia. The winners would win the Bledisloe Cup and become Tri Nations Champions.

Another shot of the same game where I was under tremendous pressure.

In Pretoria before the South Africa v Australia match. They were playing for the Nelson Mandela Cup. In this game I shook hands with one of the most famous men in the world – the giant, Nelson Mandela.

The presenters of *Bwrw'r Bar*: Rowland Phillips, me, Jonathan Davies, and Eleri Siôn.

Refereeing New Zealand v South Africa in the Tri Nations.

Giving Ireland a penalty in the 6 Nations match at Croke Park against France. A great match that was a privilege to be part of.

Many have said I needed glasses. Well I had plenty here to choose from in the Specsavers photoshoot celebrating the company's on-going sponsorship of Magners league referees.

School visit to Coedcae school Llanelli to talk to pupils about homophobic bullying and my experiences of being bullied in school and coming out. I am an ambassador of the Excellence Centre Wales, a charity workshop that helps young gay and bisexual people.

Launching Macmillan Cancer charity school sports fundraising day with pupils from Ysgol Dewi Sant Llaneli. (My cousin Cory Owens is the one waving to the right of me.)

In 2009, the 'Bloodgate' scandal hit the headlines, and as you can see, I was the referee, trying to get some order on the touchline. If I had seen Tom Williams wink and spit so much blood out as was caught on camera I would have checked further and not taken the word of the Harlequins medical staff.

(Photo: David Rogers, Getty Images)

Lining up for a team photo with my team of officals before the 2009 Heineken Cup final at Murrayfield.

Lining up for the national anthems with my two assistant referees Tim Hayes and Allain Rolland before the South Africa v New Zealand test match in Durban. Always a great moment for any referee. And to stand and watch the All Blacks do their Haka is always a moment to savour.

Sending J P Pieterson, the South African winger, to the sin bin for a high tackle.

After the South Africa v New Zealand match in Durban this year I was on the front and back page of their national newspaper on the same day. I wonder how many Welshmen can say that.

On the front page, I was having a smile off John Smitt after awarding a penalty; on the back page, I was in a good position to award Morne Steyn's try.

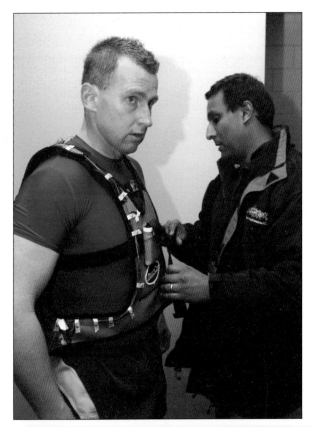

Getting wired up with the communication system before a Tri Nations match in Hamilton New Zealand. Some say I look a bit chubby on TV when refing, my excuse is this contraption I have to wear underneath my jersey for the match.

With Cerys and Elis my little cousins at my book launch.

Speaking at the National Library of Wales Aberystwyth about *Hanner Amser* the Welsh version of this book with Librarian, Andrew Green.

With Shane Williams, Eleri Siôn, Jonathan Thomas, Gwyn Elfyn and Gethin Jenkins who all came along to help me launch my Welsh book last year and raise some money for cancer research.

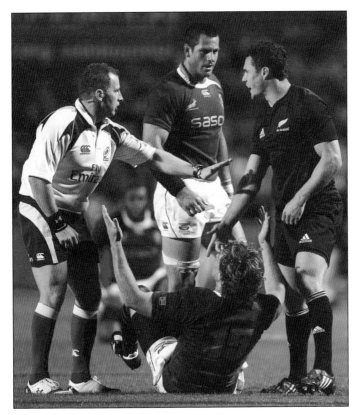

Trying to cool Dan Carter and Francois Steyn down during a heated moment in the New Zealand v South Africa match in Hamilton, 2009.

(Photo: Hannah Johnston, Getty Images)

A welcoming moment, especially after a hard intense match, blowing the final whistle!

(Photo: Sandra Mu, Getty Images)

sometimes without needing to do so. Once we were all in a pub in Swansea when a group of lads began to point towards me and seemed to be talking about me. Then they started walking over, but before they got to me some of the Pontyberem boys, Darren Goddard, Willis and a couple of others blocked their path. 'What's the problem? What's going on here?' they asked, anticipating some aggro. However, the lads' explanation took them by surprise. I had apparently taken them on a rugby course and they'd been discussing amongst themselves whether I'd mind if they came over to have a word with me. Yet it was good to know that I had such loyal friends.

I've had many opportunities in recent years to undertake broadcasting work and I must say that I've enjoyed every one. I appeared regularly for a time on the children's Welsh language programme *Rygbi 100%*, presented by Sarra Elgan, in which Dwayne Peel coached youngsters in various aspects of the game and I explained a different set of laws every week. It was a thoroughly enjoyable programme to be part of, but very different to *Jonathan*, and I am grateful to Emyr at Cwmni Da for the opportunity.

As a viewer I'm attracted to all kinds of programmes except reality shows, particularly programmes like *Big Brother*. Having said that, I was a regular follower of the show when Glyn Wise and Imogen Thomas appeared on it. I was so glad to see both giving the Welsh language such a high profile on an 'English' channel and, as a result, it seemed at the time that speaking Welsh was the 'in' thing to do. Their contribution proved to be of much greater benefit than that which many a national body has endeavoured to achieve over a much longer period.

Presenting radio programmes, especially when live, has given me as much pleasure as working in television. I had my first experience of this as a presenter on the Radio Wales programme *Out in Wales* some time ago, which gave me an opportunity to wander here and there, chatting with various people as I went. Then in 2008 I was asked by Sian Gwynedd, the editor of Radio Cymru, our Welsh language radio service, whether I'd be interested in doing some regular radio work. I replied that I would be delighted to do so but that my rugby duties at present would prevent me from making any such commitments. Yet I was given the opportunity to present a live programme on Radio Cymru every day for one week while the regular presenter Marky G was on holiday. This was a slot which had once belonged to the great Ray Gravell. I really enjoyed the experience and was very grateful for the assistance I was given by BBC staff such as Tomos Morse, Bethan Jenkins and Keith Davies.

What appealed to me about live radio was that it made me feel as if I was in the kitchen in the company of the listeners and talking to them face to face. So much so that sometimes when I was reading a link, I half expected someone to answer me back. I was really thrilled to realise that people had turned on their radios to actually listen to me, yes me, Nigel Owens, the lad from Mynyddcerrig. I got quite a few telephone calls from people telling me that they had enjoyed my stint and complimenting me, particularly on the varied selection of music that I had chosen. Who knows, after I've finished travelling the world to referee rugby matches, I might perhaps have other opportunities to do live radio. I very much hope so.

As I have already noted another radio experience I had recently was to front a series of four programmes for Radio Cymru, produced by Telesgop and called *Cynnwrf Y Clwb* which featured the activities of the Young Farmers movement in Wales. During the programmes I would follow members of a few Young Farmers clubs as they pursued their interests while preparing for various competitions and the Royal Welsh Show. It was a very enjoyable experience, particularly since being part of the Young Farmers activities once again brought back so many happy memories for me.

When I was small, although I liked performing, it was never my intention or wish to appear on radio or TV, so that has come as a kind of bonus. Yet I have to confess that my favourite place to perform is still on stage. I would have been happy enough if my career as a comic had been limited to appearing in local variety shows and I would be loathe to see that aspect of my public life coming to an end. But I realise that it was the experience and the pleasure that I got from appearing on stage that ultimately led to my getting opportunities to enjoy other areas in the entertainment world, and that the confidence I derived from performing locally from an early age has enabled me to step easily onto the public stage of international refereeing.

CHAPTER 10

Internationalism

THE IRB TRIES TO prepare promising referees, namely those whom it thinks will eventually take charge of international matches worldwide, by having them referee games in the Under-20 World Cup (which replaced the Under-19 and Under-21 competitions). They are also asked to officiate in the IRB World Sevens Series which reaches its climax with the World Cup competition. I followed that path from 2001 to 2005, and there is no doubt that it was at these tournaments that I started making the right impression on and off the field in order to progress onto the bigger stage of international refereeing. In that respect I'm very grateful to Steve Griffiths, who used to be in charge of IRB referees, for his support and guidance. The Sevens tournaments gave me a chance to see the world. In all I took part in thirteen of them, refereeing in eight finals. Although that particular form of rugby requires the referee, as well as the players, to be exceptionally fit, the fact that one was able to spend leisure time in exotic places like Hong Kong and Dubai was a very pleasant bonus.

Apart from the fact that Sevens matches usually provide a feast of open rugby, they also give players and officials an important opportunity to get to grips with some key areas of rugby in a more leisurely context. One of the most important elements of modern rugby is the tackle area. If a referee can master that aspect, particularly at the fifteen-a-side level, then the game will flow that much better. A referee must also ensure that he has his wits about him in Sevens rugby, because any mistake he makes can lead to a try in an instant.

My performances at that level must have been satisfactory, since I was then given the opportunity of refereeing international matches at senior level. The first occasion was up at Pittodrie, the home of Aberdeen Football Club in May 2005, when Scotland played the Barbarians. The following month I took charge of the game between Japan and Ireland in Osaka. I didn't feel all that great going into those two games because I was battling with all kinds of emotional problems. I knew that I was gay but, for various reasons, I had to conceal it almost continually. I was also trying to get over a relationship that had just finished. I was not in the right frame of mind to referee international rugby matches; I was asking myself if I even wanted to be in that position at all. Those were the only two games I have ever refereed when I was conscious of the fact that I felt nervous and apprehensive as to whether my performance was up to scratch. Derek Bevan always said that 'a good referee is a happy referee'. His words certainly rang true at that time for I didn't referee particularly well in either of those matches, mainly because I was unable to concentrate on the game. The two touch judges in Osaka, Huw Watkins and Nigel Whitehouse, were fully aware of my predicament and since they were also familiar with some of my personal problems, for example that I had just 'come out' and that I disliked travelling long distances, they gave me considerable support.

I didn't enjoy my visit to Japan as much as I should have because I was feeling so down. However, it made a lasting impression on me. The people were so kind and their welcome so warm that I found it hard to reconcile their hospitality with the atrocities which that nation had committed during the Second World War. (By the same token, one wouldn't have thought that Argentina had fought such a fierce war with Britain some twenty years previously, judging from the excellent welcome I received in that country.) Also, everywhere I visited was so clean and their public services, such as the railway system which runs so punctually, were very efficient.

In September 2005 the IRB Refereeing Panel met to select the referees who would be taking charge of the autumn internationals. Following that meeting I took a call from Paddy O'Brien, who had just taken over as the IRB Elite Referees Manager from Steve Griffiths. Being in charge of the sixteen IRB referees, as well as the IRB Touch Judge Panel, Paddy was responsible for informing us of our appointments and discussing any issues regarding our refereeing performances. Early one September morning I had a phone call from Paddy informing me that I was the referee who obtained the lowest marks for the season – based on those two games in Scotland and Japan. Consequently I wouldn't be refereeing any of the sixteen internationals which would be played that autumn. I decided there and then that I would not allow things to get me down in future, or worry what other people were going to think of me. You can only control the controllable, and my refereeing performances were in my hands. It was up to me to convince the powers that be that I was good enough to referee at international level and that I perhaps deserved another chance. All I needed to do was sort myself out and put in the performances on the field.

After a few weeks I got another call from Paddy, asking me to take charge of a game arranged at short notice between Argentina and Samoa in Buenos Aires that December, with Huw Watkins and Rob Dixon of Scotland running the line. The assessor for that match was Dougie Kerr, also from Scotland. I thoroughly enjoyed it because I was in the right frame of mind. I was also determined to give it my best shot, since it was possibly my 'last chance saloon'. I refereed the game pretty well in terribly wet conditions, and I was so pleased that the assessor gave me such good marks for my performance. That game changed my whole attitude and I very much hoped that, as a result, I would be allowed once again to join the hierarchy of international referees.

That's exactly what happened, and I was given similar opportunities in 2006. During the summer I was asked to referee the final of the Churchill Cup in Canada. That year the tournament had been contested between the New Zealand Maoris, Canada, the United States and the 'A' teams of England, Scotland and Ireland. The skipper of the victorious Maori team, who defeated Scotland in a very exciting final, was Paul Tito (who now plays for Cardiff Blues). What made the occasion so special for me was that other referees had been required to take charge of the previous rounds but I had been invited to fly out to Edmonton just to referee the final.

I then went back to Argentina to take charge of their World Cup qualifier against Uruguay. What I recall more than anything about that visit is that the weather conditions in Buenos Aires during the game were atrocious. Indeed, they were so bad that it was agreed not to bother with the national anthems before the kick-off. I got good marks from Carlos Molinari, the Argentinian assessor, who was a shrewd old character. There's no doubt that my profile as a referee was considerably enhanced as a result of that game, for I was then promoted to the ranks of the Six Nations Championship referees.

In October 2006 I was asked to referee my first big game in the Heineken Cup, between Leicester and Munster. Although I had refereed a few matches in this competition already, this was the chance I had been waiting for. Many other officials and former referees in Wales thought I deserved such an opportunity in order to start establishing myself as one of the top referees in Europe and then, hopefully, the world. It was a very tough match between two giants of European rugby and one that had a lot of interesting talking points, notably a match-winning penalty right at the end. I refereed pretty well, with the result that the report and feedback I received were very favourable.

At the beginning of the 2006 season I was also appointed

to referee one of the autumn internationals: Italy v Australia. For that game I was assessed by Bob Francis of New Zealand, one of the IRB referees selectors. I was very grateful to him for good marks and extremely valuable advice which served me well in some testing matches that lay ahead.

Early in 2007 I reached the pinnacle of my career up until that point: refereeing one of the matches in the Six Nations tournament. I took charge of England against Italy at Twickenham – a game which the home team won comfortably (20-7), mainly as a result of the reliable boot of Jonny Wilkinson. But perhaps my abiding memory of the day, which was a very important family occasion for us, is an incident which occurred off the field.

My parents had come with me to London and were staying with my cousin Louise. My father accompanied Paul, Louise's boyfriend and Keith, her father, to the game while my mother went shopping with the ladies. When I looked up at the main stand during the anthems I was surprised to see that the three men were seated right above the tunnel, and that just four places away from them were Rob Andrew and Prince Harry. What gave me an even greater shock was seeing my father sing the English national anthem with such fervour, which was something I hadn't imagined he would ever do. The occasion appeared to have got the better of him! Yet I remember saying to myself at the time, 'I bet he hasn't got a clue that there's a member of the royal family, who happens to be third in line to the throne, sitting four seats away from him.' So after the game I went up to my father in the bar and asked, 'Did you realise who was sitting near you?'

'Yes,' he said, 'I had spotted him.'

'Who was he then?' I asked.

'Well, Rob Andrew, the old England outside half and his son.'

I'll never forget the expression on his face when he heard who, in fact, 'the son' was. I was so glad that my father had been able to be there, for the occasion had meant a lot to him as well as me.

My mother never came to see me referee and only rarely watched me on TV since she felt so nervous on my behalf. Neither did she like to hear of supporters calling me nasty names and would not take kindly to commentators or pundits criticising my performance during a game. Like every doting mother, she thought her lad could do no wrong! Yet during the last year or so of her life she watched every match I refereed live on television. Maybe that was why I put in such commendable performances during 2008. I was determined to make her proud, particularly since I knew that she wouldn't be around much longer to watch and support me.

If I required tickets for family members or friends at Twickenham I would contact one of the administrative staff called Kate Saddler, who always looked after us very well. Referees are also looked after in similar fashion in Wales by Marcia and Stacey, the administrators in the referees department at the WRU. In fact, if it wasn't for them, I wouldn't know where I am half the time.

On the refereeing front there were bigger occasions on the horizon. The following July, I was chosen to referee the final game in that year's Tri Nations series between New Zealand and Australia in Auckland. It would be my first visit to New Zealand and I was looking forward to it immensely. It was also my first Tri Nations match and, having refereed only seven internationals up to that time, I suppose I was comparatively inexperienced for a game of that magnitude – especially in the eyes of the New Zealand and Australian media. This was the biggest match of the summer because the victorious team would win the series and the Bledisloe Cup. As if to add an extra buzz to the occasion, the game was the last for both teams before they took part in the 2007 World Cup. They were expected to announce their respective squads to go to France a few days after the match.

The tension and the atmosphere before the game was electric, as reflected in the press. At such times I like reading the local newspaper coverage in order to get a feel for the importance of the occasion in which I shall play a central part, while not allowing anything I read influence the way I will referee the match. I don't, however, read the newspapers with the same enthusiasm after a game. I know full well when I've had a bad game and I have no need for a newspaper journalist to tell me that. By the same token I also know when I've had a good game and in that respect one of the best indicators is the reaction of the players themselves. As it happens, I've learned that the press write about the referee only if he's had a disappointing match; if he has a good game he scarcely gets a mention. If the press have cause to praise an open game and a number of exciting tries, there is rarely reference to the fact that it was partly down to good refereeing.

Until 2007 coaches could request a meeting with the referee on the day before a big international match, in order that they might question him as to his interpretation of various laws. However, such meetings were often just a vehicle for coaches to complain about some of the tactics used by the opposition. On the Friday before the All Blacks v Wallabies encounter, both teams asked if they could meet me for a chat. I had quite a shock to discover who, and how many, from the New Zealand camp came to see me, namely Graham Henry, Steve Hansen, Mike Cronn (their expert on tight forward play), Wayne Smith (the backs coach) and Richie McCaw, the captain. A small, informal gathering, as it were!

The basic aim of the meeting in their eyes was to tell me how I should referee the tackle area. They were worried because South Africa and Australia had been complaining that Richie McCaw wasn't being penalised often enough for killing the ball on the floor, and that consequently I would be looking to do that regularly. They also wanted to know what I'd be looking out for in the scrum. Meanwhile, John Connolly, the

Australia coach, was worried that, in the light of all the media talk about Australia's apparent scrummaging weaknesses, I would be too ready to penalise his team every time the scrum collapsed.

All I did, in each case, was to inform them that I never went into a game with preconceived ideas as to what and when I was going to penalise. I stressed that my decisions would never be coloured by what I'd read in the press or what I'd heard on radio or television. My policy was to referee only what I saw before me. Both factions seemed happy enough when we parted company. Although that kind of meeting was then prohibited during the World Cup and for the following two seasons, it has since been reintroduced for various reasons, but on the understanding that only one coach per team could attend. Every referee has his own view on whether these meetings are worthwhile or not. Personally, I don't have any preference at all and, in some cases, I have found such meetings to be very interesting. This was particularly so of the ones I had with Martin Johnson and Peter De Villiers before the England v South Africa match I refereed in November 2008.

I learned soon enough that some coaches had little regard for the referee as a person. Their aim in these meetings was to get the referee on their side or to discover some weakness in him as a person and as a referee. If they won the match he would be the best referee in the world, but if they lost he was usually the worst referee ever. Most coaches have no qualms about crucifying the referee in the press and the media if it avoids having to take the blame for losing a game. John Connolly, a coach for whom I have the greatest respect, was a good example of this. I took charge of the game between Bath and the Ospreys at the Liberty Stadium in 2006. The visitors won and in the post-match press conference, Connolly, the Bath coach at the time (and former Swansea coach) remarked that it had been so nice to have a referee who was completely unbiased, despite the fact that he was operating in his own back yard, as it were. He added that he thought I would go on to have a very successful career. A few years later, when refereeing the New Zealand v Australia encounter, I penalised Sterling Mortlock for a high tackle during the second half. Dan Carter kicked the resulting penalty for the All Blacks, one of many successful kicks for him that day.

Connolly was under pressure following some disappointing performances by Australia, and after the game he announced that I was the reason his team lost. He went on to say that some of my decisions on the day indicated that I was too ready to favour New Zealand since they were the home side. On reviewing the match afterwards, I realised that the tackle wasn't high and that the penalty award should not have been given. In fact it was the touch judge who made the call, as I was unsighted at the time. But the fact remained that it wouldn't have changed the outcome of the match in any way, and I got a really good report from the assessor, who was also an Australian. In any event I was happy with my performance on the day. The most important thing for me as a referee is that when I blow the final whistle, the team that should have won actually did so, and that no wrong decision on my part had a bearing on the outcome of the match.

I have been disappointed over the years with the attitude of some coaches and players whom I considered to be my friends, but that's another story – which I'm sure will be told when the final whistle is blown at the end of my career. However, I should emphasise that I have the greatest respect for many coaches, particularly those who are willing to accept the referee's decisions, win or lose.

To return to the Auckland match, since both teams had been whinging so much about each other in the build up, the local newspapers had been keen to do an interview with me in order to reveal how I was going to address that particular problem on the field. However, I refused since I didn't want to speculate as to what *might* happen. My job was to referee what I saw during the eighty minutes. So I had quite a shock to see the headline in one of the local papers on the morning of the game. It read: 'Gay Ref to Blow the Whistle on Bledisloe Decider'. The article contained nothing of a nasty nature but it was rather laughable that that headline seemed to suggest that my being gay was one of the game's most important aspects!

The previous night I watched a television programme at the hotel on Jack Nicklaus. He spoke of his last appearance in the British Open at St Andrews when, on witnessing such a supportive response from the large crowds on the final few holes, he thought to himself, 'This is why I have chosen to play golf professionally, so I'm going to make sure that I enjoy every second of this special occasion.' When I walked out for that game in Eden Park and saw the crowded stands and all the passionate supporters, I remembered his words and told myself, 'This is what it's all about!' I, too, was going to enjoy every minute of this wonderful experience to the full. And that's what I did, and have tried to do each time I referee, no matter which match or how big or small an occasion it might be. Yet I have to admit that, rightly or wrongly, the bigger the occasion, the better I seem to be prepared and therefore the better I perform.

I had a good game, although I didn't get every decision right. At one point New Zealand were pressing hard and looked likely to score a try. But the ball went loose and I blew up for a knock-on, whereupon Richie McCaw protested that in fact the ball had been knocked back by one of the Wallabies. I said, 'I'm sorry, but from where I'm standing it looked as if one of your players knocked the ball forward. If I'm wrong, I apologise.' 'OK,' replied McCaw, and he seemed to accept the explanation without any qualms. I must add that, in my experience, players seem to appreciate honesty in a referee. As it happened, when I looked at a recording of the incident it showed that McCaw was right. But since the All Blacks won the game quite easily in the end, I heard no more about the incident. It might well have been a different story had New Zealand lost. As with many things in life, referees also need a little luck from time to time.

Although 2007 had been a successful year for me, I didn't think that I'd be chosen to referee in the World Cup in September. I had perhaps earned my place amongst the top sixteen IRB referees but only twelve would be selected for the 'big one'. I wasn't even certain of being chosen as a touch judge. However, it was eventually announced that I'd been chosen as a referee and was therefore, by implication, considered to be one of the top twelve referees in the world. My hopes of doing well in the tournament were high. I also took great pride from the fact that I was the only referee to be chosen from Wales, thus ensuring that the custom of having at least one Welsh referee at every World Cup, since the inception of the competition in 1987, would continue. I took charge of three games in all: Georgia versus Argentina in Lyon, Scotland against Romania at Murrayfield and the match between Fiji and Australia in Montpellier.

In truth, I was a little disappointed that I didn't get an opportunity to referee a match between some of the big guns or one of the quarter-final games. Yet, bearing in mind my position some fifteen months previously, I was grateful that I'd been given an opportunity at all. I was quite pleased with my performance in the pool matches and I got good reports for all three games, especially the first one between Argentina and Georgia, for which my assessment from Steve Hilditch, a very wise and pleasant character from Belfast, was as good as that given to any referee throughout the competition.

There's no doubt that I climbed a few places in the referees table as a result of the World Cup, for I was asked to take charge of two games in the Six Nations the following season: France v Ireland and Italy v Scotland. I got to referee the latter match because Joel Jutge, the likeable and excellent French referee, had to pull out after sustaining an injury from which, sadly, he never recovered. He was forced to retire in 2009 and will be greatly missed, not only as a referee but also as someone who was great company off the field. I also took charge of New Zealand v England during the summer of 2008. New Zealand won quite comfortably but it was a very difficult match to referee. I had some stick in the press afterwards from England's Rob Andrew concerning the fact that I was staying at the same hotel as the All Blacks team. He obviously thought that this had influenced my refereeing of the game, which I can assure you was not the case – or ever will be. When you travel abroad to referee, it's the home country's rugby union that is responsible for your accommodation. In New Zealand and South Africa, you can find yourself staying in the same hotel as the teams. It is therefore wrong for someone to criticise the referee for staying at the same hotel. It was even more unfair to accuse me of bias because nothing could be further from the truth.

During the World Cup, I also acted as a touch judge, a fourth official (who would serve as the reserve referee), and as a video referee. It was as a video ref that I suffered my greatest embarrassment during the tournament. The referee for the quarter-final between South Africa and Fiji in Marseilles was Alan Lewis. At one point during the game, the Springboks had crossed their opponent's line but Alan wanted confirmation from me that a try had been scored. On looking at the incident in slow motion on the video, it seemed immediately obvious that it was a try. The conversation went something like this:

'Nigel, can I award a try?' asked Alan. I answered, without any delay, 'Alan, you can award a try.'

'Nigel are you there, can you hear me?' asked Alan again. 'Yes, Alan, I can hear you,' I said. 'You can award the try.' But Alan asked me a third time. By this time I'd realised that something was wrong and that Alan hadn't heard me at all. I looked down and my heart missed a beat when I realised that I hadn't activated the switch on the mike which enabled Alan, and the viewers at home, to hear me talking. To the 80,000 spectators who saw the incident being replayed in slow motion on the big screen at the ground and to the millions of viewers watching at home, it was so obvious that South Africa had scored a try. Yet they must have all thought that this experienced video referee was having difficulty in coming to a decision on such an elementary matter. I apologised and later explained that there were sound problems which had interfered with the radio communication between me and Alan!

The referees' base during the World Cup was in Paris, apart from when our duties took us to other locations. We had a great time there and enjoyed socialising as a group. Many of us were old friends who had earned our spurs together on the refereeing circuit over the years. Wayne Barnes, Dave Pearson, Bryce Lawrence (from New Zealand), Craig Joubert (South Africa), Simon McDowell, Malcolm Changleng and myself all came through the system together and we remain good friends to this day. The only other Welshman on duty during the 2007 World Cup was Huw Watkins, who is great company as well as being a good tourist. Indeed, I got on well with all the referees and touch judges at the World Cup and still maintain close contact with many of them and I always have a text message before any big matches from Tony Spreadbury wishing me the best of luck.

We had some very memorable dinners together in Paris and by that time it had become common practice at the end of an evening to drag me to my feet so that I could give a song. In one such dinner at a restaurant on the banks of the Seine, held for the referees, their partners or wives, and members of the referee's selection panel, I sang 'Myfanwy'. When I sing this plaintive song at concerts it usually results in some of the audience shedding a tear or two and this was the case on that particular evening, with even Paddy O'Brien getting a little emotional. But perhaps the most important social custom in

Paris was that a few of us would meet in Tony Spreadbury's room each night for a cup of hot chocolate before retiring.

The tradition of my having to render a song began years ago at the Hong Kong Sevens. During a dinner for players, officials and the press, someone from each country represented had to go on stage to sing a song, and I was commandeered to do so on behalf of the referees. I have to confess that I have never been so nervous; my knees were trembling. I knew that there were one or two players in the audience who, having been on the receiving end from me in the past, were looking forward to seeing me make a fool of myself. I didn't have a clue what I was going to sing but I ventured a few notes of a familiar and melodious Welsh hymn, 'Mi Glywaf Dyner Lais.' After a few bars another voice joined in from the back of the hall. It was the broadcaster Wyn Gruffydd who was on duty with S4C. We got an amazing response which culminated in a standing ovation.

During slack periods between matches, particularly at the end of the pool games, we were allowed to return home for a while. I went once, for three days, to see my parents and to record a programme in the *Jonathan* series. The families of referees and touch judges were also given an opportunity to come over to Paris for a while. I had a great time in the company of Chris White and his family: wife Lynne, who comes from Garndiffaith; their son Deri and daughters Rhiannon and Siân – all the children, of course, having lovely Welsh names.

I became big mates with Siân although she was just nine years old. She was quite a character and rather mischievous, just as I was at her age. When Chris asked her after returning home what she had liked most about Paris, she apparently replied, 'Nigel Owens, Daddy.' When I accompanied the family on a tour of some of the Parisian sights we visited Notre Dame. There you could donate two euros to obtain a candle, which you would light before offering a prayer. I gave Siân the required sum so that she could do precisely that. When she returned, smiling broadly, I asked her what she had requested in her prayer. She shyly admitted that she had asked for England to win the World Cup. 'What?' I exclaimed. 'I can't believe that I've donated money to see that happen!' Wales, however, were out of the competition by then so I didn't really mind who was going to win. Perhaps that's the main reason why I'm an international referee: I am completely unbiased. But only when Wales aren't playing, of course!

CHAPTER 11

Challenges And Changes

I WOULD BE THE first to admit that the life of a professional referee is very enjoyable. However, like most other careers, it has its disadvantages. In my experience, these are represented by the disastrous overseas journeys which occur from time to time.

In February 2006, Nigel Whitehouse, Huw Watkins and I travelled to Moscow to officiate in a preliminary World Cup tie between Russia and Spain. We were due to depart from Heathrow at 1.30pm on the Friday, allowing us sufficient time to get to Moscow that night in readiness for the match the following afternoon. Huw and I travelled up to London on the Thursday night so that we could collect our visas from the Russian Embassy when they opened the following morning. When we got there, we were told that the visas would not be ready until late that afternoon. Cue panic! The check-in desk for our flight was due to close at 12.30 and we had to meet Nigel at the airport at midday. We telephoned Clive Norling and informed him of the problem. We hoped that something could be done to get our visas processed more quickly or, if necessary, to change our flight time. However, Clive's only advice was, 'Tell them who you are and make sure you are all on that flight, or else!' Eventually, staff at the WRU office persuaded British Airways to keep the check-in open until 12.45 and we managed to obtain our visas by 12. What followed was a crazy taxi ride across London, during which the driver went through several 'no entry' signs, over many pavements and through an occasional red light in order to get us to the airport on time.

We had been sitting in the plane for half an hour when it was announced that it was snowing heavily in Moscow and that since the plane's wipers were faulty, they would have to be repaired before we could take off. We waited for one and a half hours for this work to be done, but in vain. We were then told that a replacement aircraft was being flown in to take us to Moscow, which was followed by a second announcement declaring that no replacement aircraft could be found and our flight would have to be cancelled. So, after two hours on the tarmac, we were escorted back to the departure lounge. We now had to try and get another flight out to Moscow as soon as possible. The only other available flight was the last to depart that night, with the Russian airline Aeroflot. By the time we got to the counter to make our reservations there were only three seats remaining. We were very relieved, even though we realised that we would have to wait around all day. We spent the time walking about the airport and trying to get an hour or two's sleep in a quiet corner somewhere (which we didn't achieve). Then, around midnight, we boarded the flight to Moscow.

I have been on a few bad flights in my time but this one took the prize for poor standards. The service was terrible, no one on the flight deck spoke English and the plane itself seemed to be in poor condition. I was quite surprised that it managed to get off the ground without falling apart. After we had landed, a chap sitting behind us got up to open an overhead locker, whereupon a large box fell out and landed on Huw's head. He was rather shaken for a second or two, then jumped up to give the culprit a piece of his mind. But when he saw that the man was about 6ft 8ins tall, he sat down again quickly without saying a word!

From the airport we were taken in an uncomfortable transit van through the snow to our hotel in the centre of Moscow. It was now about 7.30 on Saturday morning and, with the game due to start at 2.30 that afternoon, we needed to put our heads down as soon as possible. After some three hours sleep we got a wake-up call so that we could travel to the stadium, a journey which took one and a half hours through the grey streets of Moscow. By the time we arrived at the ground it was snowing much more heavily but we decided to get changed into our official match gear. We were hoping that the match could get underway before the weather deteriorated but it began to snow so heavily that the game was cancelled.

We were then taken to a building nearby for a reception which should have taken place that evening. It was 2pm and unfortunately there was only one drink on offer: vodka – a very strong vodka at that! After a few glasses, things started to warm up and the Welsh contingent decided to sing a song or two. Before long all the players had joined with us as well as match commissioner John Ryan, the former Welsh team coach (who fortunately for him had flown over with a different airline to us). So the afternoon turned out to be rather enjoyable after all!

After a brief rest back at our hotel, Nigel, Huw and I decided to walk to the city centre to see some of the famous sites around Red Square and to sample some of the nightlife. We hadn't gone very far when Nigel slipped in the snow and seemed to have twisted his ankle. He was in so much pain that I had to carry him back to the hotel on my back where, with difficulty, I convinced him that he needed to see a doctor. His ankle was now very swollen and he was in a great deal of pain. After quite a while a doctor arrived and suggested that he should go to hospital for an x-ray, as he thought that his leg might be broken. After a great deal of persuasion (by which time Huw had got tired of waiting and had gone to bed), Nigel agreed to the doctor's advice. After waiting another hour an ambulance arrived, looking more like the small white fish vans that come round Pontyberem once a week selling New Quay mackerel.

After a journey which took nearly two hours, due to the

heavy snow, we arrived at a hospital which at first glance looked more like Alcatraz. On the way in we could see people lying on beds and on blankets on the floor or wherever else there was room. We passed one chap who was obviously in a lot of pain, but by the time we'd come out he had died in the corridor. Neither was he the only one lying there covered with a blanket from head to toe. Nigel's leg was x-rayed on a machine similar to a photo copier then put in plaster. We arrived back in our hotel at six o'clock on the Sunday morning and then left for the airport at ten to catch our flight home.

But there was still more bad news to come before we left Russian soil that fateful weekend. Because Nigel's injury had been incurred so recently, the lady on the BA check-in desk informed him that he wouldn't be allowed to fly for another 48 hours. Fortunately he was spared that punishment by using all his negotiating skills as a senior police officer, maintaining that he had the plaster on his leg on the outward journey! After arriving home he went to his local hospital to confirm whether the condition of his leg was satisfactory. The Moscow plaster had to be removed and replaced with another, which he had to wear for six weeks, since the original was considered to be unsuitable for that type of fracture. In other words, the plaster had not been put on properly the first time! The match between Russia and Spain was rearranged some months later but the Welsh trio didn't volunteer to officiate!

Yet that wasn't the worst overseas trip I've ever been on. That prize goes to Santiago, where I went to run the line in a game between Chile and Argentina. My airline ticket stated that I would be flying on the Wednesday night from Heathrow to Sao Paolo, in Brazil, which was a one-hour refuelling stop, before proceeding to Buenos Aires in Argentina where I would catch a connecting flight to Santiago. While we were on the runway at Sao Paolo, we were informed that there was a technical problem and, although it would be remedied fairly easily, we would have to wait an extra hour. It was then confirmed that the fault had been repaired but that a special piece of equipment would be needed to test that it was working properly before we could safely get airborne again. After waiting on board for another hour it was announced that since the equipment in question was only available at Heathrow, it would be impossible to transfer it to Sao Paolo within a reasonable period of time so our flight would have to terminate there. We were then escorted from the plane and transported to a hotel near the airport whilst other arrangements were made to get us to our final destination.

By this time it was Thursday afternoon and we were informed that we should reassemble in the hotel foyer at nine o'clock that night, since arrangements had been made to fly us to Buenos Aires during the early hours of Friday morning, and then onwards to Santiago. I had only been in bed for half an hour when the phone rang. Apparently three of us were to be flown to Buenos Aires earlier that evening. So I jumped out of bed, quickly gathered all my belongings and boarded a special bus which took us to the airport. However, when I arrived at the check-in desk some hours later, the arrangements had been changed once again. I was now to be flown directly to Santiago the following morning. I returned to the hotel to snatch a few hours sleep before getting up at 4am on the Friday morning to catch a 6am flight from Sao Paolo to Santiago.

I'd managed to get a message to the WRU asking them to inform the rugby authorities in Chile of my delay, but worse was to follow. As I sat in the departure lounge at Sao Paolo at 5.30am awaiting a boarding call, I heard the following tannoy announcement, 'Due to adverse weather conditions this airport is now closed and all flights cancelled until further notice.'

I finally flew out some eight hours later and arrived at Santiago at about 8pm on the Friday night, where a car was waiting to take me to the hotel. At last it appeared that my nightmare journey was over – that is, until my chauffeur tried to start the vehicle! He was greeted with that dreaded 'click,

click' sound which indicated that the battery was completely flat. I was stranded at the airport for two hours before someone arrived with a new battery for the car. I arrived at my hotel at 10.30pm after a journey of 52 hours from Heathrow.

The game between Chile and Argentina was being played the following afternoon but it was just as well that I was to officiate as a touch judge; I'm sure I would have been in no condition to referee. The ground in Santiago was very small but was in one of the most beautiful settings for a rugby match I have ever seen, with the magnificent Andes mountains providing a spectacular backdrop. A short time before I embarked on that eventful journey I happened to speak with Robert Warner, a very pleasant man who was president of the RFU when England won the World Cup in 2003. It appeared that we had both departed for Santiago from Heathrow at about the same time, except that his flight went via Paris. He had arrived at Santiago one and a half days before me!

To confirm the fact that travelling abroad to referee is not as glamorous as some people imagine, I should note that we usually travel Economy Class. The only time officials are allowed to enjoy the luxuries of Business Class is when the flying time is of more than four hours' duration. That's just as well, or travelling for some 26 hours to New Zealand, for example, would be a real nightmare. Yet we sometimes come across celebrities from the world of sport who travel in far greater style than we do.

I particularly remember one flight from Heathrow, via Paris, to the south of France, where Richard Hughes, David R Davies and I were to officiate in a match between Agen and Montauban in the European Shield competition. David was an experienced referee and Richard a real character from the rural village of Llandysul, in Cardiganshire. He naturally had a great interest in rugby, but apart from rallying I don't think he had much regard for any other kind of sport. Our seats were in the front row of the economy section and it was obvious from the fuss that the cabin crew were making that someone rather important was about to take his seat in the last row of the business section, just in front of us. It was Sven Goran Eriksson (along with his partner, Nancy Dell'Olio), who'd just had a very encouraging start to his career as manager of the England football team. He noticed that we were rugby officials and soon struck up a conversation with us, being interested to know why we were going to France. I happened to have a joke book with me to read on the flight, since I needed some material for a TV show that I would be doing for S4C shortly afterwards, and I'm pleased to say that Sven graciously agreed to sign it for me.

After I'd sat down Richard asked me, 'Who was that chap who was talking to us?'

'You don't recognise him, do you?' I replied.

'Well, he does look familiar,' said Richard.

'That's Sven Goran Eriksson.'

On seeing that this information hadn't really registered with Richard, I added,

'You haven't got a clue who he is, have you?'

'Of course I do,' replied Richard, 'he's the bloke who owns the Eriksson mobile phone company. I'm going to have a word with him now. It's about time they built another mast in Llandysul because the reception there is bloody rubbish!'

I only just managed to stop him from giving Sven a talking to!

That trip was memorable for another reason. After arriving in France we discovered that Air France had managed to lose all our bags, which left us with just the clothes we were wearing. Consequently we had to buy new clothes and borrow rugby kit from the Agen players to officiate at the match. The jerseys we were wearing may have been a different colour to the home side's rugby shirts but they still had the Agen name and logo on them. This didn't help David when penalising the away side!

Our luggage finally arrived two days after we'd returned home. Ever since that experience I try not to fly with Air France and try to avoid having a connecting flight from Charles De Gaulle airport – although I have had to a few times and my luggage has always arrived.

Foreign travel by road can also cause problems at times. When Robert Davies, Hugh David and I shared a taxi to Rome airport, having refereed a game between Roma and Connacht, the driver kindly went a little out of his way to show us some of the sights. As we drove alongside a railway, the driver mentioned that the city's railway system had been constructed under the direction of Mussolini. I innocently asked whether there were monuments to be seen around the city in honour of Mussolini's achievements, whereupon the taxi screeched to a halt and its three perplexed passengers were deposited at the roadside. The driver apparently detested Mussolini and anyone who sang his praises in any way! I still recall Robert's poignant advice as we stood there looking all forlorn, 'Nigel, when we get into another taxi, for God's sake don't mention Mussolini or we might never get home!'

Professional referees have cause to meet up on occasions other than those directly connected to match duties. Each October, sixteen of us assemble at the Lensbury sports club (near Twickenham) to meet with Paddy O'Brien, the referees managers from their respective countries, other officials from the IRB and the selectors responsible for selecting referees for various matches. While there, we discuss any problems which might have arisen during the previous season and any forthcoming changes in the laws, under Paddy's guidance. Usually recommendations for changes are submitted to the IRB by the unions of each country. In Wales, the Laws Sub-Committee debates and recommends any changes to the WRU board before they are submitted to the IRB. That body consists of Gerald Davies as chairman, myself, Robert Yeman, Gwyn Jones, Geoff Evans, Clayton Thomas, our national coach

Warren Gatland and Mark Taylor. We don't meet all that often, although we have done so more frequently in order discuss the Experimental Law Variations (ELVs – introduced in 2008) and decide on the way forward with regard to the ones we as a union want to keep. Apart from the ELVs and the occasional directive from Paddy and the IRB on how certain areas of the game should be refereed, changes are only introduced every four years or so whereas at one time they used to be implemented more or less on an annual basis.

Recently, before the commencement of the Heineken Cup, referees and coaches meet up – usually in the country where the final is to be played that season. The purpose is to ensure that referees will be consistent in their interpretation of certain aspects of the game, and for coaches to know what style of refereeing to expect and to raise any qualms they might have. Similar meetings are held before international games and at local and regional levels. Every referee in Wales belongs to one of the nine societies which generally meet once a month and cover the North, Mid, South, East and West regions. Three times each season, James Jones (the other professional referee in Wales), David R Davies (the former international referee who now works for the WRU as their Community Referee Development Officer) and I go along to these meetings to present different training topics and offer explanations on various aspects of the laws which are often a bone of contention; for example, the tackle area or the scrummage.

Things were a little different at the beginning of the 2008-09 season since a number of new laws were introduced. Therefore, August and September 2008 were busy as we visited each society as well as ten rugby clubs in Wales to talk about the infamous ELVs. They were introduced as a result of a number of recommendations made by a special commission set up by the IRB to improve the game. Our Laws Sub-Committee looked at the suggested changes and reacted positively, as did most of the northern hemisphere countries, to most of the recommendations. Although we were of the opinion that there wasn't much wrong with the game as it stood, we accepted that some of the proposals would be beneficial.

One change that caused much dissent was the decision to penalise many offences in the tackle area with a free kick, as opposed to a penalty kick. This rule was tried out in the Tri Nations series during the summer of 2008 and it was obvious that it was the cause of many problems. Fortunately this wasn't one of the ELVs introduced on 1 August 2008 although a few countries, like Australia and New Zealand, were strongly in favour. They considered that it would speed up the game and make rugby more attractive to watch. With that in mind, a rule forcing the three-quarters to stand five metres behind the back of the scrum was also adopted. Yet, interestingly enough, statistics from early games played under the new laws showed that they hadn't led to more tries being scored or to more clean breaks when compared to the pre-ELV period. Although some games appear to be more attractive as a result of the new laws there is still far too much aimless kicking in the game for my liking, but I don't think this has much to do with the new laws but more to do with the way the game and players are coached these days. Unfortunately this is now a prominent feature of so many matches that I feel we have to address it in order to get the exciting runners back to the fore in our modern game.

Another change which originally led to much discussion was the law which allowed the taking down of a maul. Some were in favour of the new law and argued that it was high time that the boring and persistent use of the rolling maul, which some teams thrived on, was stopped. So, last season, players were allowed to bring down a maul by grasping the opposition between the midriff and the shoulders (which of course prohibited anyone from employing the dangerous tactic of diving into a maul to grab hold of legs and feet in order to bring it down). I was opposed to this change because I didn't think it would have any great effect. Teams that had previously made frequent use of that manoeuvre would be sure to find ways of ensuring its continued success and of denying the efforts of the opposition to bring the maul down. After all, if Wales were winning 6-5 against England at Twickenham and chose to cement the victory with a series of endless mauls, I wonder how many Welsh supporters would then complain that it was a boring tactic?

There is another important consideration with regard to the maul. Rugby is a game for everybody, regardless of their shape or size. Changing that law could dispense with the previously vital contribution of the 20-stone player in the village team. What must be remembered is that the rules are there for the benefit of every player at every level of the game, and whilst the professional player might have the time and the resources to change the shape and the condition of his body to be stronger or quicker (often to satisfy changes in the laws), the lads in the village team are unable to do so. As it happened, that change lasted for one season only, so it is once more prohibited for players to engineer the deliberate collapse of a maul.

In 2009 some of the ELVs were removed and others introduced as law. There are many different views on what should have happened, but at least now everyone is playing to the same laws throughout the rugby world – apart from the odd one at various levels of the game. But more on that later.

From the referee's point of view some changes made things more difficult. For example, he would have to try and ensure that the three-quarters were standing on a line no nearer than five metres from the base of the scrum whilst still trying to keep an eye on what was going on in the front row. On the other hand, the change allowing any number of players in the line-out, within certain confines, meant that the referee didn't have to make a body count each time. However, that ELV did not become law. At least I am able to draw on the cooperation of the assistant referee during line-outs, while the poor referee at the lower levels had to sort it all out himself. I had a taste of that problem right at the beginning of last year and, although it was just at the Cwmtawe Sevens tournament in Pontardawe, it was still hard work. Incidentally, I think that was the very first time that the new laws were put into practice in Europe.

It was important that competitions of the kind in Pontardawe, along with friendly matches, were held before the proper season started in order that players and referees could become acquainted with the new system. In addition I held many discussions with coaches and players and visited clubs like Carmarthen Quins, Cydweli and Pontyberem, as well as attending meetings with some of the regional sides. Their response to the changes was very positive and it was hoped that players, supporters and referees would derive even more pleasure from the game.

CHAPTER 12

A Year To Remember

IT COULD BE SAID that, as a referee, the 2008-09 season was my most successful yet. However, off the field it was the most harrowing year I have ever experienced, due to my mother's terminal illness and her eventual passing. Yet the most difficult period for me was early in 2008 when we were told that, since the cancer had spread to various parts of her body, there was little hope that she would live for more than twelve months. Typically of her, she had been informed some days earlier at the local hospital of the seriousness of her condition but delayed telling my father and I until such a time as she considered appropriate. In fact, she and my father made sure I went to referee the crunch Heineken Cup match between Munster and Wasps, even though it was a few days after I had found my dear uncle Ken dead. It was also during the time she was in hospital with what my father and I thought was just some gallstone trouble.

After returning from Limerick that weekend and going straight up to Mynyddcerrig to see her, since she had by that time been discharged from hospital, she informed my father and I that she had cancer. At that point I felt that I had run into a brick wall and I cried for days afterwards. I was numb and didn't know what to think or do. One thing I did realise was that my father and mother needed me more than ever. However, I needed them too – to try and help me come to terms with what was happening to us as a family. For the rest of that week I stayed with them rather than being on my own in Pontyberem. I can honestly say that this was the worst time in my life. The troubles I had been through prior to that seemed so trivial.

The realisation that I was going to lose someone whom I loved so much and to whom I owed so much really hit me hard over the next few days and weeks. After all, you will only ever have one mum.

A year can seem like a long time in many contexts but when you know that you are going to lose someone very dear to you, it's surprising how quickly time passes. My mother made great efforts to disguise her suffering, but as the year wore on she became gradually weaker. The last time she was well enough to leave home was in November 2008, when she made the effort to be present at the launch of my autobiography in Welsh at Pontyberem Rugby Club. I was so glad that she could be there and I know that she really enjoyed being among some 400 other people, many of whom were family and friends. I was pleased and surprised that so many people, far more than I or anyone else had expected, had turned up for the launch to make it a truly unforgettable evening. A large percentage of the money raised that night from book sales and a raffle were donated to Cancer Research. I would like to thank Gethin Jenkins of Cardiff Blues, Jonathan Thomas and Shane Williams of the Ospreys, the lovely Eleri Siôn and Gwyn Elfyn, who MC'd the evening so well, for giving up their valuable time and coming along to support the occasion. I am extremely grateful to them all and to everyone else who was present.

After that, my mother seemed to make a special effort to witness the coming of Christmas. Over that period I spent as much time as possible in the company of my parents, although I wonder whether I could have spent more time with them – my mum in particular. On Christmas Day her youngest sister Petula and her daughter-in-law Kay cooked dinner for the three of us and brought it up ready to eat. My mother stayed downstairs until late afternoon when she announced that she was returning to bed. I then realised that she was now very ill; indeed, she was confined to her bed for the remaining few days of her life. Although her death was something I had been anticipating for many months, it was still a huge blow. Yet it was a strange feeling: a feeling of not wanting her to go but realising that she was in a great deal of pain and was unable to fight anymore. I didn't want her to suffer any longer. The final few days of someone who is dying of cancer is not something I would ever wish to witness again.

Yet there were many comforting factors. My mother received excellent care from her local doctor, Goronwy Jones, the Macmillan nurses and everyone at the cancer treatment centre at the West Wales General Hospital in Glangwili, who ensured that her final days were as comfortable as possible and also from members of the family who are too many to name, for all they did for us during the very difficult last few days of this wonderful life. Also, so many called round to express their condolences that the house was filled with people all day and every day, which certainly helped us in our grief. I was surprised that my mother's death had touched so many. This was underlined by my father and I receiving well over 1,000 cards and letters expressing sympathy.

The night before my mother's death, whilst my father was downstairs, she asked me to promise her that I would look after and care for him for the rest of his life. She knew that I would have done so anyway and I'm pretty sure she told my father that he was to look out for me as well. She also informed me that she had left instructions for her funeral arrangements in a box downstairs and asked that I follow them as closely as I possibly could. The following night, 2 January, just after 11 pm, my mum passed away. I had been by her side all evening until about 10pm, when I whispered to her quietly, whilst holding her hand, that I was going home to walk the dogs before putting them in their shed for the night. I asked her to wait for me and said that I would be back within the hour. I wish to God that I had waited a little longer. When I returned, I ran straight upstairs only to learn that she had peacefully passed away just before I arrived. I will never forgive myself for not being there the moment she died, but at least she was not alone; my Dad and his sister, Eiry, were with her.

In the early hours of the morning I opened the box in the company of my cousin Helen, who had driven all the way from Aberaeron, to find that my mother had planned every last detail of her funeral, from the moment she would leave 8 Maeslan for the very last time until she was finally cremated, after a chapel service at Capel Seion where she had been so faithful over the years. The funeral itself was, of course, a very emotional day but it was of great comfort to my father and I to see so many people at the chapel and in the service at the crematorium. There must have been over a thousand mourners there if not many more – in fact the road outside the chapel was lined with people who couldn't get inside.

I would like to thank everyone who helped me and my father through that difficult time, especially Emrys who, until the funeral, stayed up nearly every night with my dad until the early hours of the morning. In fact, on a few nights neither of them slept at all but sat talking about old times. I am also grateful to family and friends, whom I can't start to name as there were so many of them, who were a rock to us both. I am indebted as well to the wonderful people from the close community of Mynyddcerrig who did so much for us during that most difficult of times. I thank you all truly from the bottom of my heart.

There were some difficult times during the immediate aftermath of my mother's passing. I had been particularly worried as to how my father would cope in the ensuing months, especially since he now would have to attend to his own welfare and to the running of the house. However, he has managed remarkably well and is always able to draw on the assistance of the family, particularly Matthew, one of his nephews, who sees to his needs on a regular basis since I am away from home so often on refereeing duties.

Not a day goes by without my thoughts turning to my

mother. I am what I am today mainly because of her influence and the values that she and my father instilled in me from an early age. I have always tried to be aware of the difference between right and wrong, of the importance of treating people with courtesy and respect, and of the need to be honest in everything I do. That is her legacy.

I know it would have been her wish that I continued with my refereeing duties as soon as possible after her death. So one week after the funeral I went to Ireland to take charge of Munster against Sale in the Heineken Cup. I appreciated the fact that many of the players from the home side came up to me to express their condolences, and also Dwayne Peel, who hails from my locality, and a number of his Sale colleagues. I realised, however, that I had to make a special effort to concentrate 100 percent on the job in hand, regardless of how difficult that might be. The outcome was that I received a mark of nine out of ten from the French assessor, Patrick Robin. It's the highest score you can possibly have for a match, as no referee is perfect enough to get a ten. Yet I'm sure I came pretty bloody close that night, as there was no way I was going to let my mum down.

A week later I was back in Ireland, at Croke Park, to referee their Six Nations game against France. It turned out to be the most entertaining match of the championship, with the home team winning 30-21. What made it especially pleasing for me was that all the pundits agreed that it was an excellent game with no complaints whatsoever, from players or the press, being levelled at the referee and the assessor on the day, Tappa Henning from South Africa, said in his report that this was as good a performance as he had seen from a referee at this level. It was my first visit to Croke Park and I must say that the whole experience made a great impression on me.

By this time the ELVs had been in operation for a few months, and some of them had been on trial for almost four years. At the end of March I attended a meeting in Lensbury for some sixty senior stakeholders from the international rugby community, consisting mainly of coaches, administrators and a couple of ex-referees, to evaluate their effectiveness. I expressed the view that I was in favour of most of the proposed changes, since, in my experience, they appeared to have made rugby a better game. However, I stated that there were some amendments, favoured in the main by the southern hemisphere countries, which seemed to be politically motivated and were geared to try and attract spectators to the sport as opposed to making intrinsic improvements to the game itself. For example, as I have previously stated, the maul is an important facet of the game and to try and dilute its effectiveness by allowing it to be pulled down, as countries not traditionally schooled in the skills of mauling were keen to do, would be a mistake. I was glad, therefore, that the recommendation of the meeting to prohibit pulling the maul down was ultimately approved by the IRB and is now incorporated in the laws.

Yet there are still some problems which need to be resolved, such as the continuous barrage of high kicks from one end of the field to the other which is a feature of so many games. Of course some countries, such as South Africa, have adopted this tactic very effectively and their recent successes will probably make them unwilling to approve any new legislation which might limit their current style of play. Nevertheless, there are some in authority who are concerned that this is a very unattractive and boring feature of the modern game. I am unsure as to what steps can be taken to improve the situation, apart from referees being requested by the IRB to be more strict in the application of the law which requires players to retreat from an offside position and not to advance at all until they are put onside when the ball has last been played by a member of their own side.

During the 2008-09 season I seemed to have been involved in more than my fair share of controversial rugby matches, but their notoriety arose from events with which I was not directly concerned. For example, on 12 April I refereed the Heineken Cup quarter-final between Harlequins and Leinster, which subsequently became renowned for the so-called 'Bloodgate' incident. This rocked the very foundations of English and world rugby. The repercussions of Tom Williams chewing on a capsule to feign a blood injury have been far-reaching and the consequent reverberations will no doubt continue for a long time.

During the match, I recall being told that Williams had a blood injury and would need to leave the field. I could see that he was 'bleeding' and was told that Nick Evans, who had left the field earlier, would be coming on in his place. However, before I could allow him to do so, I had to check that when Evans was originally taken off, his card had noted that his removal was a 'substitution' and not a 'replacement', in which case he would be allowed to return in place of a player coming off because of a blood injury. Having been satisfied that the rules had been observed in that respect, I allowed Evans to come back on.

Some would say that I should have known that there was something up when Evans, who had limped off the field earlier, was waiting on the sidelines to come back on. I suppose I had my suspicions but I didn't see anything untoward taking place, and I certainly wasn't qualified to ask Williams to open his mouth so I could see if he had a cut or not. Maybe, with hindsight, I should have done that, but I think things of that nature are best left for the medical people to sort out. After all, what if he was coughing up blood as a result of internal bleeding and I refused to let him leave the field of play because I could not see an open wound? I felt, therefore, that the best course of action for me was to take the word of the medical person attending him that it was blood and to allow him to leave to receive treatment.

The first I, or my assistants, knew of 'Bloodgate' was when the fourth official at the match, who is primarily involved with overseeing substitutions, came to our changing room to show us a sample of Williams' 'blood' that he had managed to acquire. He had gone to these lengths because he had been suspicious, with the result that he then took the matter up with the appropriate authorities. It snowballed from there!

As I have already stated, in my opinion, taking action to determine whether a player's blood is genuine or not should not involve the referee at all. That would be a medical matter, for which the referee is not responsible or qualified in any way. In the case in question I believe we, the match officials, had taken the only possible action available to us and therefore were not to be held accountable in any way for that sorry affair. Apart from the fact that I was asked by the Heineken Cup authorities to submit a report on the incident, which I did, I have not been party to the repercussions that have resulted from that game; nor was I asked to take part in any further investigations.

Claims have been made in recent months that the use of blood capsules has been prevalent for some time at all levels of the game. I have to say that I have never witnessed such a practice – but that does not mean that it hasn't occurred in any games in which I have officiated. It certainly serves to underline how difficult things can sometimes be for referees.

Many would say that 'Bloodgate' was no different to the practice adopted by some teams of opting for uncontested scrums. For example, if they are receiving a battering in the scrums, they might ensure that a couple of the front row 'get injured' and that they are unable to replace the specialised position. Also, one player asked me what the difference was between Andy Haden jumping out of the line-out against Wales, pretending to be pushed and thus indirectly winning the game for New Zealand, and the Harlequins incident. But the business of introducing blood capsules, or deliberate blood-letting by players to cover it up (which apparently also occurred during 'Bloodgate'), does seem to take cheating to another level.

Personally I think that the matter has been dealt with correctly. I also would like to think that, if there were a Haden-type situation today, he would be cited and dealt with for bringing the game into disrepute. Well done the FA, I say, for dealing with footballers who take a dive and try to cheat their way to a penalty. I think there is a huge difference between playing fairly while pressurising the referee, pushing the laws to the limit, and cheating. However, it's certain that the authorities will have to act to prevent this happening again. Maybe the solution will be to have a qualified medical assessment of any dubious blood injuries on the rugby field.

I returned to Croke Park on 2 May to take charge of the Heineken Cup semi-final between Leinster and Munster. This was an even bigger event than my first visit to the ground some weeks previously. I also refereed the final some weeks later, but the semi was better. There was a tremendous sense of occasion in Dublin during the weekend of the match. The city was awash with red and blue flags, and on the day itself over 83,000 spectators crammed into Croke Park. This was a world record attendance for a non-international. The atmosphere was electric and the tie proved to be a thrilling encounter which Leinster won, contrary to many expectations, 25-6. There was a chance this year that the Blues and Ospreys could have played each other in an all Welsh semi-final at the Millennium Stadium. This would have been great for Welsh rugby and a real boost for our regions in the Heineken Cup, but whether we would have a sell-out like the occasion in Croke Park I am not so sure. We really are falling behind as far as attendances in our regional matches are concerned and it is something we as a nation need to address. When you look at the big crowds that attend the matches in the Guinness Premiership, the Top 14 in France and the three main Irish provinces we really have some catching up to do.

However, there was a lot of controversy after the match. Following evidence presented by the citing officer, the experienced Munster back row forward Alan Quinlan was suspended for twelve weeks for gouging Leo Cullen, the Leinster captain and lock. Neither I nor my assistants, Nigel Whitehouse and Huw Watkins, had spotted the offence during play, but had we done so I would have immediately issued a red card. As a result of his suspension, Quinlan was withdrawn from the British and Irish Lions party to tour South Africa. This was unfortunate, because I think he is a shrewd, tough forward of the old school and would have been invaluable in countering the physicality of some of the South African teams.

The issue of gouging raised its head again during the Lions tour, when Schalk Burger was sent to the sin bin for 'interfering' with Luke Fitzgerald's eyes during the second test. The incident had been spotted by Bryce Lawrence, one of the assistant referees. He then informed the referee, Christophe Berdos, who issued Burger with a yellow card. There is no doubt that if the incident had been seen properly by the officials concerned, they would have sent him off. It is very easy for someone watching slow motion replays two or three times at home to come to a decision. But to see it in actual playing time on the field and in a huge pressure-match situation is totally different. In fact, whilst viewing the game at home, I didn't see the incident as it happened but only during the replay. I don't know how I would have reacted if I had been officiating in that match. It would, of course, depend on what exactly I saw, but there is no doubt that if I had seen it clearly then I would have sent Burger off.

On 23 May I was at Murrayfield to referee the 2009 Heineken Cup final between Leinster and Leicester. To be asked to take charge of a Heineken Cup final, as I was for the first time in 2008 for Munster v Toulouse at the Millennium Stadium, made me feel very proud; mainly because it confirmed that I was recognised as one of the leading referees in European rugby. To be awarded a second final, a year later, was something very special indeed.

Some critics have said that the game at Murrayfield was a disappointment in the light of the two thrilling semi-finals, especially following the drama of the penalty shoot-out at the Millennium Stadium between Cardiff Blues and Leicester. It is also claimed that Murrayfield is unable to generate as good an atmosphere as some of the other leading stadiums – unless Scotland are playing there, of course. However, I enjoyed that second final even more than the first. Not only do I think it was actually a better game of rugby but by then I knew exactly what to expect from the occasion, was more experienced and consequently more relaxed during the game.

Referee assessments are sometimes not part of such occasions, but the unofficial feedback that I received after both games suggested that I refereed the first final well but my performance at Murrayfield was even better. The match was quite tense, with Leinster winning by just three points, but there didn't seem to be any ill-feeling or grievance towards the referee at any time. At the end of the game, players from both sides came up to shake my hand, including Martin Corry, who wasn't in the Leicester squad that day and was retiring at the end of the season. He is a true gentleman and I always respected him as a great player and captain. He was always a pleasure to referee. Only one player refused to shake my hand that day: Julian White, the Leicester prop.

While on the subject of match venues, I have often been asked to name my favourite stadium. In fact I have more than one because they each have their particular attributes. The Millennium Stadium is right at the top of the list because of its unique atmosphere, created from the close proximity of the spectators to the field of play. It is even better when the roof is closed. Twickenham also has special significance for me; mainly because it is there that I refereed my first Six Nations match. The fact that it can house over 80,000 spectators creates a special sense of occasion in itself. Of the foreign locations I would choose Stade Français, mainly because of the unique response of its spectators to events on the field. It is somewhere I always enjoy visiting. I have only run the line at Newlands in Cape Town, but the fact that the ground holds only 49,000 spectators means that the spectators there, too, are very close to the action, which in my opinion creates a very special feeling.

One of the highlights of my career occurred during the summer of 2009 when I was one of three referees from the northern hemisphere to take charge of a Lions match during their tour of South Africa. The Lions were playing the Southern Kings, a new team that was hoping to become a franchise in the Super rugby set-up. I was disappointed with the standard of my performance that day and, although I didn't referee badly, I think I should have done much better, especially in the contact area. It was a hard match during which the home team played a physical game and were continually 'on the edge'. In other words, the line between being robust and being dirty was very thin as far as their style of play was concerned. On the other hand, neither were the Lions a team of angels! Yet, mainly for the reason I note below, any foul play which might have been going on was difficult for me to spot. Some of the Lions players alluded to a number of 'cheap shots' adopted by the Southern Kings but none of their actions were cited by the citing official. Indeed, I saw incidents in some of the other Lions games which were far worse than anything which occurred in this match, and I think that press reports of dirty play were somewhat exaggerated.

I was disappointed with the assessor's report on my performance in that match. I didn't deserve to get a very good report and it wasn't his fault that I didn't perform as I should have done on the day. But I certainly don't think I warranted the poor assessment that I got. After the game we discussed the penalty try I had given and he agreed that I had been right in that respect. However, when my report came through he said it should not have been awarded. He had picked up on the fact that the Lions prop on the opposite side of the scrum to where I had been standing had slipped his bind and, in his view, may have caused the scrum to collapse. I disagree because I had specifically given the assistant referees the responsibility of drawing any such incidents to my attention, as it is impossible for me to see what goes on the other side of the scrum. Since there was no offence reported to me via our communication system, I played on and thus gave the penalty try. I still believe this was the right decision as the Lions had been forcing the Southern Kings' scrum to retreat all through the match. So, either his view of it was wrong or the assistant referee on that side did not see the offence; or, if he did, he didn't believe there was one to report.

Another reason why I was disappointed with the assessor's response was because I felt that he didn't understand my attempts to humour the players, for which I apparently lost marks. He noted a number of remarks I made to which he took exception. For example, when one player arrived at a line-out, obviously feigning injury and appearing to be on the point of wasting some time by taking a rest on the ground, I said something like, 'If you go down I'm going to penalise you,' at which point he made a sudden and remarkable recovery.

The assessor also thought I was guilty of patronising some of the players and quoted the following example to prove his point. When one of the players moved to an offside position, I said, 'If you do that again I'm going to bang [penalise] you.' He replied, 'I thought it was alright to do it,' to which I responded, 'Don't think, just don't do it!' Even the player himself smiled at the comment. On another occasion I penalised the scrum-half for not putting the ball into the middle of the scrum. 'If you're going to cheat, cheat fairly!' was my advice to him, which brought a laugh from a few of the players. Maybe it was a case of the assessor not understanding the Welsh sense of humour!

I think one of the main reasons for my below-par

performance in the Lions match was the fact that I had become too complacent and perhaps even a little too relaxed in my approach to the game. Maybe I thought that, since I was now regarded as one of the leading referees in the world, the match would be just a walk in the park, as it were. How wrong I was. One thing is certain: I learned from my mistake that day and I will not fall into such a trap again.

I set myself high standards in 2008-09 and I think I have given some good refereeing performances. However, the problem is that people expect a top-class international performance from you every game, and that is virtually impossible to ensure. We all accept that even the best players in the world are unable to perform at their best every week, yet we expect the referee to do so. I believe this is a little unfair. After all, one must remember that we are only human too! Yet, although it's impossible to referee at the peak of one's ability throughout the year, one can't afford to let standards slip as I have done in a few matches during the long, hard 2008-09 season. It's something I will be working hard on during the coming year, in order to make sure that it doesn't happen again. Indeed, that will be one of my main aims for the next season.

I spent most of my time in South Africa on my own, since my refereeing colleague Alain Rolland arrived some time after me and then, since our respective duties took us to different locations, we didn't stay in the same places. Yet I made some great new friends during my stay in Cape Town, namely Ian Badenhorst, a young man who was studying and working as a cameraman in the area and who has since been over to stay with me for a few weeks. When I returned to South Africa for the Tri Nations a few weeks later, he did some filming for a documentary that Avanti are doing on me, which will be aired by S4C before the 2010 Six Nations tournament. I also managed to catch up with friends from Pontyberem towards the end of my visit and we had a great time together. They were part of a huge Welsh contingent which, along with the notable Irish presence, underlined for me that the prophets of doom who predict that the days of the Lions tours are numbered must be mistaken.

I was at home for about two weeks before having to leave once again for South Africa. For me, the two greatest international fixtures in the rugby calendar are Wales v England and South Africa v New Zealand. I will never, of course, get to referee the former but I was really delighted to learn that I was to take charge of the second Boks v All Blacks match in the 2009 Tri Nations series in Durban. This was only the second time I had been appointed to referee in that great competition, and I considered it to be a notable honour. (Northern hemisphere referees missed out on the 2008 Tri Nations due to the fact that different ELVs were in operation in the southern hemisphere.)

South Africa had won their first encounter with New Zealand and on 1 August they had another comprehensive win against a disappointing All Blacks side. Although I refereed the match pretty well and had a good report from Michele Lamoulie (the wise old French assessor who is a great character and very knowledgeable on rugby matters), I did make one glaring mistake. This prompted Graham Henry to submit a fairly harsh coaches' feedback report to Paddy O'Brien concerning the sin-binning of Isaac Ross in particular. I confess that I got that decision wrong, although it was only after seeing the incident from another angle that I could see the ball was out and that he was well within his rights to play it. As I have mentioned before, I will hold my hand up when I make a mistake, so I apologised to him for it. Henry also cited a list of instances which, in his opinion, showed that I had been wrong in my interpretation. Most of these were refuted by both Paddy and myself, after I had reviewed them, but Henry did have a fair point with regard to a couple of the decisions he had questioned. I responded accordingly and agreed with him.

I had one more test match to referee during the summer, namely New Zealand v South Africa in Hamilton on 12 September 2009. It turned out to be a hell of a match and one that I really needed to referee well, as it was pretty much the tournament decider. There was a lot of pressure on me, not just because of the match's importance but also because I had not performed as well as I should have previously – particularly now that I was recognised as one of the six best referees in the world. I had a pretty good report from Tappe Henning, the match-day performance reviewer and the feedback from Paddy was that I had refereed the match very well overall.

There was also a lot of press in New Zealand that week about that coming game, particularly concerning the fact that Peter de Villiers, the Boks coach, had made a statement to the media that he was no longer going to meet referees the day before the match. For he was of the opinion that, with regard to previous matches, Bryce Lawrence and Wayne Barnes hadn't refereed in the way that they had told him they would. Moreover, he thought that the IRB referees had it in for South Africa because they were the world's best team. Of course, that is not the way we referees work at all. We are the best at what we do because of our neutrality on the pitch and I certainly don't care who wins when I referee a match. I am sure that all the other IRB referees will tell you the same. That controversy put even more pressure on me, but that's how I like it. As I have mentioned previously: the bigger the occasion the better I perform. And that's what happened.

* * *

At this stage I'm not sure what I'd like to do with my life after my career as a referee comes to an end. I could do more public speaking engagements and media work, give commentating a go, or try my hand at refereeing football locally in Wales or even maybe try my hand at umpiring cricket. I am a great believer that no matter what the sport is, if you are good at refereeing and managing people on the field, with training and experience, I think you could give officiating a go at the top end of the game, no matter what sport it is. Many may say that you need to have played at a decent level in that particular sport to be able to officiate at the elite end of the game, but I don't think that's true. After all, I started refereeing when I was sixteen years of age after only playing a few years of school rugby.

Who knows what the future holds for me. I may stay involved in refereeing in some capacity so I can give something back to the game that has given me so much joy and opportunity over the years. In fact, I have already started helping by giving some young referees what I hope is valuable advice and encouragement. It would be nice to think that I could resume singing 'traditional' Welsh songs on stage to guitar accompaniment, although my standard of playing would have to improve significantly first! One thing is certain: I have learned that I must try to make the most of every possible moment in the company of those who are important to me – particularly friends and family. After all, that is something which gives far more pleasure than a game of rugby.

I hope that you have enjoyed reading *Half Time*. I trust that it has given you an insight into the life of a referee at the top end of this wonderful game of ours – a team game that cannot be matched by any other sport in the world, a game for all shapes and sizes. Long may it continue that way. For those of you who are experiencing the same problems that I had to face for many years in my life, I truly hope that reading this book has given you encouragement and hope to face the future, to be yourselves and to know that you are not on your own out there. People really care about you and love you, no matter who or what you are. I hope you can now see that whatever worries or problems you may have, you can start to look to the future in a much more positive frame of mind. The most important thing I have learned is to be yourself. Don't try to be something or anyone you are not. It took me years to realise that, but after doing so life is much better, believe me.

Appendix

Places and Locations

One of the advantages of being a professional rugby referee is that I have the time and the opportunity throughout the year to visit many places in various parts of the world. Apart from the occasional unpleasant experience, I've really enjoyed travelling here, there and everywhere and I fully realise how lucky I am that I get to see the world whilst pursuing a career that gives me so much pleasure. Of course, various places leave different impressions with visitors so, often with tongue in cheek, this is my take on the places to which rugby has taken me and the experiences which came way during those visits.

Amsterdam

The city's Sevens tournament took me here. It's rather an odd place which seems to cater for all tastes. I didn't see any tulips but I noticed many flowers in the windows on offer at the right price!

Auckland

This is where I refereed my first Tri Nations match, between New Zealand and Australia in 2007. Plenty of things to do here but I was surprised that the rugby 'buzz' on test-match days wasn't greater. Many immigrants from Asia now come here to get an education.

Bath

One of the nicest cities in England. I love refereeing here because the Recreation Ground is always full, thus creating a wonderful atmosphere. There is talk of moving form the Rec to a new purpose built ground. It will be a very sad day for rugby if they do.

Belfast

I also enjoy refereeing at Ravenhill, the home of the Ulster team, since there is always a great atmosphere here. The welcome is very cordial but the city's unfortunate past is still quite evident. Yet, despite that, Belfast is still of great interest to visitors. As my tale of our experience at the Hilton illustrates, it is still possible to get into trouble if you happen to be in the wrong place at the wrong time. Old wounds remain open in some areas of the city.

Biarritz

One of my favourite places in France. It has fine weather for most of the year and its location by the sea adds to the relaxed atmosphere that's always to be found here. After saying that, last year we were stranded there for a an extra day due to the gale force storm that hit the area. But we had plenty of food and good wine to keep us entertained!

Bloemfontein

I have only been to this South African city twice. Although I enjoyed my stay there, it would be far from my first choice of places to stay in South Africa. I'm usually in and out in a couple of days if I'm officiating here.

Buenos Aires

One of the most welcoming and bustling cities I have visited, with traffic seemingly running wild! The food is excellent and prices fairly reasonable, although I was surprised to see so many poor people. Outside the city you can find some of the prettiest views in the world. I would go back there anytime.

Cape Town

One of my favourite places in the whole world and the safest city in South Africa. Seeing whales off Cape Point and visiting Robben Island, where Nelson Mandela and others were imprisoned, were unforgettable experiences.

Cardiff

Every referee in the world loves coming to Cardiff to officiate at the Millennium Stadium because of the unique atmosphere and the fact that it has such a central location in the city. Welsh people can be proud of their capital.

Christchurch (New Zealand)

This is the home city of some of the current All Blacks, such as Richie McCaw and Daniel Carter. In my experience it is a fairly cold and miserable place but the people were very friendly and, once again, rugby didn't seem to figure as prominently here as I would have expected.

Connecticut

I was here for five days and I wouldn't have been able to tolerate it any longer. I have never in my life encountered such unpleasant and rude people. To get there I had to fly to Los Angeles, where the airport staff were just as discourteous. I usually have to touch down in Los Angeles when I fly to New Zealand, an experience which I always detest. I now try to go via Hong Konv every time!

Coventry

After visiting this city, I can appreciate why the English use the expression 'send to Coventry' in connection with someone with whom they wish to have no dealings whatsoever.

Dubai

The famous Sevens competition brought me here. The weather is always fine, the people very polite and the streets safe. Drinking alcohol is not permitted in public places but there are plenty of hotels and bars where it is freely available. Anyone who starts trouble here is likely to find themselves being carted off to jail in a jiffy.

Dublin

I was disappointed the first time I came here. I was looking forward to experiencing the craic and enjoying the company of some truly Irish characters, but they have become a rare breed. It's now a huge city with many Eastern Europeans having settled here of late. Fast food restaurants are all the rage and many city restaurants even display their menus in Polish. There's still a very warm welcome and I've had many enjoyable times here, but it wasn't what I expected it to be.

Durban

The winter here is warmer than our Welsh summer, can you believe. I spent most of my time relaxing on the beach and swimming in the warm sea, which was great. The ABSA Stadium is a terrific venue for test matches. It would not be my first choice as a place to pass time in South Africa – that would be Cape Town – but it would certainly not be my last.

Every year they have one of the great wonders of the natural world: the epic Sardine Run. Billions and billions of these fish, stretching for miles long and wide, swim up the Indian Ocean. They are driven close to land by the dolphins, whales and sharks that pursue them – so close in fact that you can stand in the sea and scoop them out in buckets as they pass. In 2009 it took place too late for me to be able to witness it. The reason for this is that the sea was warmer than usual for that time of year. Apparently the sardines don't come quite so close to land anymore because of the effects of global warming. I regret that I didn't visit Rorke's Drift whilst I was there as it wasn't far away. Never mind, that can wait till the next time!

Edinburgh

A lovely city which has a special character, with the castle on the hill providing an impressive viewpoint. Yet the sun never shines when I'm there. I had a memorable New Year's Eve there with the Pontyberem lads, which made up for the extremely miserable afternoon I'd spent refereeing Borders v Glasgow.

Edmonton

The city itself is a kind of concrete jungle but the journey from there to the Rockies was absolutely amazing. The former RFU president, Robert Warner, was part of the group that travelled with me. When we were asked what our reaction would be if we came face-to-face with a grizzly bear, his reply kept us laughing for days. In his posh English accent, he said he would greet the animal with the words, 'Hello, Bear!'

Galway

My favourite Irish town. It is small and particularly homely, not unlike Carmarthen. It is the home of the Connacht Rugby Club and after each match there the stadium is given over to greyhound racing. I once placed a bet on a dog called Red Rum but, needless to say, it didn't win.

George

The home of the IRB Sevens tournament in South Africa is a delightful village between Cape Town and Port Elizabeth. Ernie Els has a home by the sea, which says a lot about the area's attractiveness. I spent many weeks there enjoying the weather, the beach and the sea. It was a fantastic experience.

Glasgow

A pleasant city with an excellent shopping centre. While I was there I got to see the Celtic stadium... eventually. At my first attempt I had jumped into a taxi and asked the driver, 'Can you take me to Parkhead Stadium, please?' At which point he slammed on the brakes and shouted, 'No f***ing chance. Get out and walk! I'm a Rangers supporter.'

Gloucester

This is a rugby city through and through and the supporters in the famous Shed stand form one of the noisiest and most biased crowds in rugby. When I referee there I always stay in Cheltenham, which is a nicer place.

Hamilton (New Zealand)

Not somewhere you would normally choose to go to in New Zealand as there are many more interesting places to visit. Yet I thoroughly enjoyed my few days there and would certainly return. The rugby stadium is as good as they get: small, but with 32,000 packed in close to the playing area. I refereed a Tri Nations match to remember here; it was the place to be that weekend. And if you like plenty of nightlife then you will be very happy here.

High Wycombe

This is the location of Adams Park, the home of Wasps. The rugby here is of the highest standard but there is nothing particularly attractive about the place. When I'm refereeing here I usually stay in Richmond.

Hong Kong

Too many people, too much traffic and smog, but a great atmosphere in the stadium for the IRB Sevens. It's the best of all the Sevens locations. This is also where I took charge of one of the games that gave me the greatest pleasure as a referee, namely the Sevens final between New Zealand and England.

Johannesburg

Provided you stay in an area like Sandton City, which is one of the city's safer districts, you will enjoy Johannesburg. There are some very dodgy areas. It was common practice to see motorists choosing not to stop at red lights in case they were mugged in their cars. I saw a person get stabbed on the street as someone tried to steal his mobile telephone. It's sad to think that life has so little value here. On the plus side, I found the food to be really great and prices in the shops to be very reasonable.

Leicester

At the Welford Road Stadium you will find the best atmosphere and this is of course the home to one of England's truly great rugby sides. Always a great pleasure and experience to referee here, but I ain't that fussed on the town itself.

Limerick

Munster's success has really put the town on the map. The stadium where they play, Thomond Park, has become a kind of fortress where it is very difficult to win. I enjoy officiating there and have always had a very warm welcome. Mind you, I haven't yet refereed there when Munster have lost. Unfortunately, Limerick is now known as 'Stab City', though I can truly say that I've always felt safe there.

London

Much too big for me, but I suppose there is always something to do.

Marseilles

Each time I have been here, in a city where soccer is much more popular than rugby, the atmosphere in the stadium has been fantastic and the weather fine. Alan Lewis, Malcolm Changleng and I once spent a whole day on the beach before officiating in an international match.

Montpellier

For me, this is the third most pleasant place in France (after Biarritz and Marseille) to referee. It is a beautiful area and it's here that I took charge of my first game in the 2007 World Cup, between Argentina and Georgia. After getting such a good assessment for that game this town will always be close to my heart.

Moscow

The whole atmosphere appears cold and grey, as do the people who live here. One gets the impression that secrets and mysteries are an intrinsic part of everyday life, as if all those years under Stalin still cast a shadow over the city. But, in a funny kind of way, that's part of its appeal.

Paris

I spent almost a week here during the 2007 World Cup. This is where the best food in the world is to be found, and sights like the Eiffel Tower and Notre Dame are well-worth seeing. But in my opinion the city is at its best at night, for during the day the streets seem quite dirty and the traffic is really bad. In 2007 I went on the Metro – my first experience of travelling underground – and got completely lost. I detest underground trains wherever they are, because I find them a cold and lonely form of transport. I can't see myself using them again in a hurry!

Perpignan

A smashing place with very hospitable people, but the rugby stadium is one of the last places I would wish to be when the home team are losing. The atmosphere is enough to send shivers down your spine since it is the home of the most fiery supporters in France.

Late in a game between Perpignan and Leeds I allowed Gordon Ross, the Leeds Tykes flyhalf, to retake a conversion which won the game for his team. He had missed with his first attempt, during which some of the Perpignan players had shouted loudly as he approached the ball. This was against the rules and completely unfair. His second kick went over and Leeds won by one point. After the match, the Perpignan coach kicked the door of my changing room open and started shouting in French. (I was able to guess what he said!) That match-winning decision made the headlines in the sporting press the following day and my name was mud in France, particularly in Perpignan! The two teams met again the following week with Huw Watkins in charge. Although Perpignan won that match he was still given a hard time, apparently because he was Welsh! He was booed even before the kickoff and this lasted until he left the stadium that evening. I haven't referee out there since that particular incident but I'm sure to go there sometime in the future, and were I required to make a similar decision again I would do so! One thing is certain: I would not be likely to receive the warm welcome I had experienced on my previous visit.

Port Elizabeth

I was told by a few referees that there was not much to do here, therefore I stayed only two nights. However, the only forgettable thing about this place was my performance in the match. I should have stayed longer as there were plenty of things to do and see in the area. From here you can take what they call the 'Garden Route' and drive back down to Cape

Town, staying a night or two in different towns en route. It is, apparently, one of the most beautiful drives you could ever wish to undertake. If I ever get the opportunity to go there again, I will certainly make the most of it and drive along the Garden Route.

Pretoria

If you ever go to South Africa, do your best to avoid this place. It's not safe to go anywhere on your own and I saw a few people getting mugged. But the rugby stadium, Loftus, is one of the best and most intimidating in the world.

Rome

I spent a very pleasant time here. There's so much history to enjoy. For example, standing on the spot where it is believed Julius Caesar was murdered and visiting the Vatican gave me quite a thrill. A very expensive city nevertheless.

Rovigo

Known to us in Wales because Carwyn James came here to coach. It's not surprising therefore that Welsh people always get a warm welcome here. A very small, but great rugby town.

Santiago

Capital of Chile and quite hospitable. The location of its international rugby pitch, at the foot of the Andes, is the most beautiful that I have ever seen.

Tauranga (New Zealand)

Spent three lovely days here at a hotel on the beachfront at Mount Maunganui. It's a lovely part of the country and we were looked after so well by Bryce Lawrence. I spoke, along with Wayne Barnes, at a fundraising event at the local rugby club one night and had a marvellous time in the company of great rugby people. We drove to Rotorua one day to taste the local Maori culture at Te Puke, which was a wonderful experience. However, if you go there, be prepared for the smell of sulphur which emanates from an abundance of boiling mud pools and thermal springs which are the result of volcanic activity deep below ground. If you ever go to New Zealand, especially during the 2011 World Cup, then visiting this part of the country is a must.

Toronto

The people are far more courteous than the natives of the United States. You will find some of the prettiest views in the world here. One of the most exhilarating experiences I have ever had was going to the top of the CN Tower which, at 1,815 feet, was the highest building in the world at the time. My legs were still shaking after I had come down.

Venice

A place which has received too much praise in my opinion. If you ever go there, remember to take plenty of money and a pair of armbands if you can't swim, as there's a good chance you'll struggle with all the waterways!

Victoria

During my visit to South Africa for the Under 21 World Cup in 2002 I had the opportunity to spend three days near Victoria Falls in Zimbabwe, in the company of Simon McDowell (the Irish referee), Patrick Robin (the former international referee from France and an assessor from Australia, Mick Keogh and his wife. The trip had been arranged by one of the touch judges at the World Cup, who came from Zimbabwe. We stayed in log cabins on the edge of one of the lakes at a spot where elephants, baboons and springboks came to drink each day. A fantastic area and, apart from the falls themselves, which are so spectacular, the surrounding countryside was awash with colour and wildlife.

It's hard to believe that Mugabe has allowed the country to deteriorate to such an extent. Nevertheless, the children we happened to come across seemed so happy and appeared to have permanent smiles on their faces even though they looked so poor and under-nourished. I remember one in particular, a thirteen-year-old lad called George, who tried to make some money at the roadside by selling hand-carved elephants. I was amazed by his knowledge of British history, which he had acquired from books he obtained from tourists. I asked him if he knew where Wales was. 'Yes,' he replied, 'Prince Charles comes from there.' He was fairly close to the mark but I had to correct him slightly! George could also name all the prime ministers of Britain and Australia over the last hundred years.

It was obvious that he'd had a hard life – both his brother and his father had been murdered by the cruel Mugabe regime. So when we gave him more than the asking price for some of the elephants, he grabbed hold of me and thanked us for our generosity, displaying the broadest smile I have ever seen. I must confess that I shed a tear or two at that point. I shall not forget that moment as long as I live.

In our everyday life we often complain about little things which get us down, but compared with what some people in this world have to suffer, particularly children, we have nothing to complain about. After that experience I felt so grateful that I'd been raised by a loving family, by the best parents anyone could possibly have, in a comfortable home and a civilised country.

We had a chance also, while in Zimbabwe, to walk along its border with Namibia and to go on a rather precarious boat trip on the Zambezi. I felt a little nervous as we passed by the elephants and the hippos that were wallowing in one part of the river. They seemed to be quite suspicious of us and I was seated at the side of the boat, quite close to the water. However, what made me feel even more wary was that I'd noticed there didn't seem to be any life jackets on board. So I asked the chap who was steering. 'Well,' he said, 'anyone who falls in will be snapped up by the crocodiles within five seconds, so there would be no point in having life jackets!' At that point I asked if I could be moved to the centre of the boat!

Watford

This is the home of the Saracens. Despite all the stars who have played for them over the years, the stadium they share with the soccer team is rather disappointing. The only good thing about the town is Elton John!

Wellington

My favourite place in New Zealand is 'Windy Wellington'. It deserves this description but it's a homely and very relaxed city. Yet here I had one of my most miserable experiences as a referee, as far as weather conditions are concerned. At the start of the game between New Zealand and Ireland the temperature was 16 degrees centigrade but it fell to zero by the final whistle. It was also raining heavily!

Mynyddcerrig

I cannot include this place in any alphabetical order. Need I say more? This the best place in the world. This is where everything started and, some day, maybe, this is where everything will come to an end.